Bear Attack SEO For Managed Service Providers
Scott Millar

Copyright © 2018 IT Rockstars Ltd
ISBN 9781729382721

Contents

Acknowledgments	4
Chapter 1: Is SEO the Silver Bullet?	5
Chapter 2: Topics and Keywords.	13
Chapter 3: Content Strategy & Planning	26
Chapter 4: Content Creation	37
Chapter 5: Content Promotion	46
Chapter 6: Let's get technical	55
Chapter 7: What not to do	69
Chapter 8: Hacking the Map pack	75
Chapter 9: Backlinks	90
Chapter 10: Website Layout	99
Chapter 11: Adwords	109
Chapter 12: Brand Jacking	120
Chapter 13: Press Releases	131
Chapter 14: Measuring Results	139
Chapter 15: Build to sell.	150

Acknowledgments

I'd like to thank the following people for making this book happen:

Gran Millar - for the £1000 so I could buy my first desktop PC and then immediately take it apart and flatten the OS. Drivers were not easy to download then! (1995)

Seona Shand - for recommending I go to an SEO conference all the way back in 2007- this started my passion.

Carol Benzie - being patient with me and giving me the space to learn all about Citrix and server infrastructures.

Mr Neil Stewart (Portlethen Academy) - I hated English but he made it very enjoyable.

CCarter - Wickedfire/Builder society. For inspiring my digital marketing activities in his epic posts.

Rob Hamilton (Dynamic Edge Group)- Allowing me to switch from the techie to the sales role and the opportunity to work with a great team.

Jacqueline & Aurelia - giving me the space to complete this work.

My mother spotting the errors in my spelling book (Primary 5).

Google - for the easy rankings when I needed them.

Special thanks to my American Mom for editing this book.

Chapter 1: Is SEO the Silver Bullet?

SEO for MSPs is not the silver bullet that will solve your MSP sales strategy.

Not all of your leads are searching Google to find your services, so don't make that assumption.

Building relationships and referral networks (offline) matter more than any form of online marketing, if you are in B2B IT sales.

But...there's this book...

From an online perspective, SEO is the most effective way of acquiring a qualified lead online and should not be ignored.

Why is this?

Unlike social media marketing, SEO allows you to be in the buyer's mind at the correct point in the sales funnel.

They are actively looking for something you have to offer.

You can get your website in front of the right customer at the right time.

You can't do this through social media.

Enter the qualified lead.

The Qualified Lead

Qualified lead generation is crucial to growing a business. It not only helps your sales team win more business, but also reduces the amount of time talking to unqualified leads.

SEO is a qualified lead generation marketing channel.

How much is a qualified lead worth to your business? Let's say for example you have ten leads of which you have a conversion rate of 33%. Out of those ten leads, three will become customers.

Now let's assume we generate $1000 per month over the course of a 36-month contract for the average MSP customer. Including monthly recurring revenue, project work, and hardware. That's $108,000.

Take those initial three leads that turn into sales and the math states every qualified lead is worth almost $32,400 for your business.

If this book helps generate only one lead, it is worth your time to invest in the steps outlined in this book. So, commit yourself to do it.

Bear attack?

The title of this book is "Bear Attack SEO". This is not just some gimmicky name to poke your interest.

If there was a crowd of people and a bear attack was imminent, you only have to be 1% faster than the slowest person in the crowd to survive.

The same is true on the 1st page of Google. If you only give 1% more effort than your competitors, and you will be on top.

That's the basis of this book. Putting in that extra 1% effort (which is not much) to outrank the competition on the search engines.

My Story

Before we get stuck in, it probably would be worth telling you about my experience in the SEO business. I am a systems engineer at heart, but in my early years had a passion for video games.

I made the switch to SEO when I realized that SEO was just another game played with the search engines, but with a financial reward.

I got stuck in SEO back in 2007 when it was o-so-easy to game Google. A handful of backlinks pointed at your website, and you could pretty much be guaranteed number one position for any locally based keyword.

When I realized this, I put it into action, starting my own computer repair business – a part-time venture which quickly grew due to all the leads and calls I was getting thanks to SEO tricks.

These were, of course, just tricks. Google got smarter and I got greedy. At the height of the games, I had three businesses. I got my fingers burnt badly in the years of the "penguin" and "panda" Google algorithm updates. (More on this later)

I then started work for an MSP transferring my skill set as an IT manager of a 600 user based infrastructure and repair tech to the world of the MSP. A few years down the line, I began a different challenge; business development for an MSP aka sales.

I had one big problem with sales. I could easily pick up the phone and cold call. Meet with directors of companies and convey how we could transform their business using technology. Talking about technology and closing the sale was easy. My problem was leads.

Based in Aberdeen, Scotland, (the Oil capital of Europe back when the oil crash of 2014 was in swing), no one was considering upgrading their IT. It wasn't only the oil business. Almost every business was affected by the downturn in some way.

Leads were scarce. I felt certain that I could utilize my SEO skills to help get over the bump and generate qualified leads. However, I had a bigger problem - the chip on my shoulder.

I'd worked hard with the team I'd been part of for four years. Moving to business development and the opportunity to open the sales funnel to more leads would increase the business significantly. I planned to do it on a national scale. My boss was great. He gave me the opportunity to move from the engineering role to sales, which was a risk financially to his business. I, however, had my own perspective.

If I'm was going to drive all this new business, I should have some ownership in the company. This was a non-starter. My boss did not want to dilute the company shares any more than it already had been.

I could continue in my role and enjoy the extra commission, but I was thinking long term. I looked at my superiors who had been with the company longer than myself, and were only a few years older. They had nothing to show for their hard work and effort over the years apart from a pay check at the end of every month. I was not going to make the same mistake.

My only option was to quit the job and go it alone.

IT Rockstars was born.

The plan in my head was to compete with my old employer in precisely the same services. I quickly designed and developed a website that was soon ranking for key terms in the search.

This site started giving me a trickle of new leads every month. This was great! I had hit the ground running.

After a few months servicing clients I had an epiphany. If I can make lead generation work when the local economy was on it's knees imagine what type of response I'd have in other locations.

I realized I did not want to run an MSP. I know how much hard work is involved. My passion was search engine optimization.

Why not combine my knowledge of the IT industry, my move from break-fix to MSP, and the ability I have to rank and optimize websites for search engines.

Applying my knowledge of SEO, sales and tech experience made me decide that this book had to be written for the IT community.

Expert?

I'm not going to go into too much detail. But it's safe to say I've been doing this long enough now I know what works and what to avoid. You know how the saying goes, an expert is someone that has made every mistake in the book.

If you stick around, I'll tell you about the time I was a pure black hat SEO that was reborn as a white hat SEO.

I must point out now that this book is purely white hat tactics of SEO.

There is no point risking something as important as your business website to a Google algorithm change. I'll be showing you how to play by the rules and tell you exactly what Google likes, and what to avoid.

How This Book is Organized.

If you are anything like me, you'll have a collection of business books; some real golden knowledge with tips, tricks, and best practices.

Excellent advice which you read but don't implement. That's certainly how I operate, so I've written this book as a checklist.

Read the chapter, perform the actions, check off from the list. It's designed to be a systemized process that you can implement in your business or delegate someone else to follow.

The first action is to download and print this checklist. I've also got some fantastic free SEO tools to help you get started and reveal exactly what some of your competitors are doing to out rank you in the search. https://www.itrockstars.co.uk/resources to grab your exclusive copy.

Timeline and Plan

Beginning today, give yourself or team twelve months to accomplish the majority of the results from this book. Patience is the principal strength when optimizing your website for search traffic.

You will be generating qualified leads, and long-term it will be something of value that can be leveraged when it comes time to sell your business (if that is part of your plan).

This book is written in a linear timeline beginning with keyword research where you delve deep into what your services are, your ideal customer, and what they may be searching.

We then cover building the foundations which include reviewing technical on page website optimization and the best practices to put in place.

Armed with your keywords/topics and the page foundation, we then cover content strategy which will form the meat of your SEO efforts.

The technical SEO is the easy bit, (which we will cover). The hard work is being consistent and having a process. The systemized process is our goal.

Finally, I'll introduce you to off page SEO processes that all go towards having that 1% gain that will see you sitting at the top of the search engines.

In finishing Chapter 1 and before beginning Chapter 2, remember:
- 1% gains are your aim over the course of following the steps in this book.
- Anything you do today, be prepared to wait 12 months to see results. Be patient.

- Don't rely solely on SEO for your leads, it's only one method and Google can't be trusted – it's a website just like any other that you don't control.

Chapter 2: Targets and Goals aka Topics and Keywords.

Keywords are like the bullseye in a firing range target.

From an SEO perspective, a keyword will form the basis of our content and website structure. You will need to figure out what keywords to target.

Once this chapter is complete, you will have a list of keywords you can implement as part of your content strategy and content generation.

The first thing you have to do is to figure out what you want to be "found for" in the search engines.

The method I have used the past is something like the Google Keyword Planner to measure search volumes.

This tool allows you to put a keyword in and spits out approximately how many searches a month in your country are performed for that keyword.

The Google Keyword Planner

Keyword ideas   🔍 IT Support London   — *Your target keyword*   DOWNLOAD KEYWORD IDEAS

Found 270 keyword ideas

☐ Exclude adult ideas

Keyword suggestions   *Monthly search volume (national)*   *Adwords Cost*

☐ Keyword (by relevance)	Avg. monthly searches	Competition	Ad impression share	Top of page bid (low range)	Top of page bid (high range)	Acco
☐ it support london	1K – 10K	High	–	£8.28	£20.98	
☐ it companies in london	100 – 1K	Medium	–	£3.28	£10.53	
☐ it support company london	100 – 1K	Medium	–	£8.24	£20.15	
☐ it support services london	100 – 1K	Low	–	£10.33	£33.40	
☐ it services london	100 – 1K	Low	–	£5.73	£12.49	
☐ small business it support...	100 – 1K	High	–	£11.20	£22.70	
☐ business it support london	100 – 1K	Low	–	£9.80	£22.44	
☐ outsourced it support lon...	10 – 100	Low	–	£6.14	£19.91	
☐ it solutions london	100 – 1K	Low	–	£3.22	£7.22	
☐ it outsourcing london	10 – 100	Low	–	£7.79	£17.07	

Google Keyword Planner

The keyword planner is excellent for specific markets, but to tell you the truth you have to think a bit smarter than going after the keywords that get the most searches that are related to your business.

The Google Keyword planner should be avoided when trying to work out what search volumes are for a particular keyword. The main reason for this is the fact that it is not accurate. (I do not know any keyword tools that are accurate).

From a managed service provider's perspective, the other reason it should be avoided is due to the low search volumes we are going to be dealing with locally.

The keyword planner does have its uses for consumer keywords that get over 10,000 searches a month. However, in a local market there are not 10,000 businesses searching for terms related to IT and managed service providers.

Focus to Gain Control

What you must do is define what earns you the most profit and is the easiest service to perform or product to sell.

Then you have to form the customer avatar, which is a detailed profile of your target customer and what he/she may be searching.

This is a winning combination. I came to learn about this combination back when I was optimizing my site for laptop repair back in my break-fix days.

If found that there might not be as many people searching for laptop repair, but I could charge more for a laptop repair at the time, just for the fact that it was a laptop and customers expected to be charged more.

I took this a step further and thought about what types of laptop repairs were easy to do and made me the most money. It turns out that laptop screen repairs were a boon.

A new screen at the time cost around $50, I could charge $250 for the full repair. The repair itself only took 15 minutes.

Once I had figured out this winning combination, it was just a matter of adjusting what my target keyword list was. I soon had a winning formula of anywhere between 5-10 phone calls per day with potential customers with smashed laptop screens.

Apply this logic to your MSP's services and products and you are on to a winning formula.

> A word of caution – the world changes, customer habits change, do not get too comfortable with a winning formula. I learned this lesson when the iPad came along and wiped out a lot of the laptop customers.

From an MSP perspective - cybersecurity has been a hot keyword but what does the future hold? If you can be ahead of the curve on your keywords and content, you will have less competition in the search results, and when that keyword does become hot, you will be on top.

To recap – Think about your most profitable service or product and how your customer would search for that. Then, base your keywords around this combination.

The Customer Avatar and Funnel

I have already given you an example of a keyword, "laptop screen repair."

That would have been a possible phrase that someone may have typed into a search engine.

There are many variations of this phrase that might be typed and for all you know they might not be ready to call someone to fix their laptop screen.

They might be higher up the sales funnel.

As an example, they might be thinking about how they can fix their laptop screen, the search here would be "how to fix a laptop screen."

In the MSP world, we usually have a good chance of winning a client over after a major incident. When they have lost faith in their current IT provider.

An example for you would be "do I pay the ransomware."

Maybe they are worried about data breach due to the ransomware "can I get sued for loss of data."

In this example, we are targeting high up in the sales funnel. These are great keywords as not only can we target potential clients that have a ransomware infection.

The IT Sales Funnel

Local IT Services sales funnel

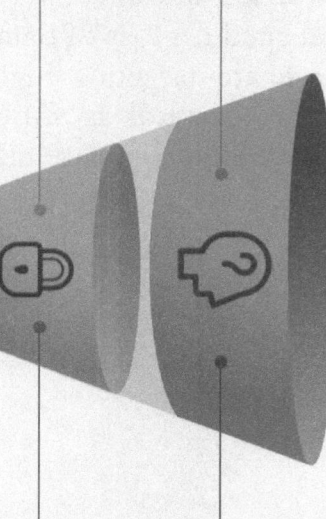

WORRIED ABOUT I.T. SECURITY
Local business owner that sees phishing emails on a daily basis. It's back of mind, they just delete the emails when they spot them.

STAFF HAVE BEEN DUPED
Staff have clicked on email phishing scams, accounts have been hacked and emails sent to address book.

READY TO SWITCH
Major ransomware attack. Current IT firm can't recover the back up and is forced to pay the ransomware.

TOP OF MIND SEARCH TOPICS
IT security training for staff, how to stop scam emails, how many scam emails should I be getting.

EDUCATED AND INFORM
Password policy, email security, stronger email protection.

TAKE THE SALE
Should I pay the ransomware, what happens if I pay the ransomware, IT/Cyber Security companies.

These lists of keywords can be endless. My suggestion to you is to keep it simple. Focus on 3-5 groups of keywords you want to rank in the search engine, and where in the funnel you want to be in the customer's mind. Once you have these keywords planned out and supporting content, Google acknowledges this, and you will start appearing for similar topics in the local results. **Please note** that I used the word "topic". Google is moving away from keywords.

Your content has to be topically relevant. Keywords are the bullseye, but the topic is just as important.

I have made this task 100% easier for you by providing a master keyword list for IT and MSP providers.

This list is based on the most common services an MSP provides.

I have broken them down into the following topics:

- IT Support
- IT Security
- Backup & Disaster Recovery
- Cabling, network and wifi infrastructure
- Server and cloud infrastructure/solutions
- IT Strategy & Management

You can download the master keyword list on the resources page at
https://www.itrockstars.co.uk/resources

Coming up with your own list:

First, select the six main services you focus on in your business and in your mind think of how your customer would search for that product/service.

Then perform a Google search on each of these keywords. At the bottom of the search results, you are given a "suggested search list", as shown in the example below.

This example list is compiled by Google on similar searches that real people have searched for. This is by far the most accurate way to come up with the way your customer would be searching on Google.

Once you've studied these suggested search phrases, you'll have a clear idea of the topic you need to be addressing.

As an added bonus, these suggested words have a good search volume so you can be guaranteed you are not generating keywords that have either none or very limited searches.

Now that you have a master keyword list here is an explanation of the thinking behind the keywords:

IT support category

Terms such as:

IT Support + location
IT Company + location
IT Services + location

One thing I would mention about this first category is that it is the most competitive, and for intended purposes, probably the last category you will rank for in the search if you have a relatively new website. The reason for this is due to its competitive nature.

Also, all the local competition wants to rank for these keywords and are actively targeting them. How can you apply the **bear attack** tactics to this situation? Simple. You outsmart the competition by going after niche relevant keywords such as:

IT support for accountants + location
IT services for recruitment firms + location
IT company specializing in nonprofit

Very few people are going after these terms, and they are highly relevant to your business. If your company is anything like the ones I have been part of in the past, there are industry sectors that sit very well in your client portfolio.

Take the top three industry types you currently support and base the IT support category around these areas.

IT Security Category

I have always thought IT security was a bit like home insurance -- The client is not interested in what is covered by the insurance until they have a fire.

The same is valid for IT security. It is something that is not actively searched that often until there is a security breach.

Let us imagine John Smith, CEO of a small recruitment consultancy has had a ransomware outbreak. The incumbent IT provider has failed, and there is no recoverable backup.

John starts searching for options online, such as:

> IT security experts + location
> Data recovery expert + location
> Ransomware recovery specialists

Whilst these types of terms will not frequently be searched, when they are searched, you have a high chance of converting that website visitor to a qualified lead.

Another example in the IT security space would be the IT manager for an organization that is looking for a penetration test on his/her network.

These types of customers always have high-value potential if you can perform an IT security audit to the correct standard. Mainly because once you have won an IT manager with one service, the other services you offer can quite easily complement each other.

I am getting off topic here, but the logic is coming back to the most profitable services you offer, remember those laptop screens?

What is a Good Client for You to Have and What Might They be Searching?

Spend some time on this question and if you are comfortable, ask your existing client base.

Disaster Recovery and Backup

This is similar to the IT security category in that you will be targeting people who have an immediate need for your services. aka bottom of the sales funnel.

Another John Smith, this time his roof has sprung a leak directly onto the server rack. The incumbent IT supplier (MR Breakfix) has quoted him a ridiculous amount to recover the server infrastructure.

It is your time to shine. Target the correct keywords with content that educates and informs (more on this later).

Here is a search that comes up which may be worth investigating further. (I did not even know this existed):

"water leak detection system for a server room"

Cabling, Network, Wifi Category

The structured cabling category crosses over with the network category, so I have combined both. Now you may not offer structured cabling services, but more than likely you work with a trusted partner. The structured cabling searches usually are higher up in the IT sales funnel.

Eventually that new network socket is going to need something plugged into it. So, even if you don't offer these types of services internally, it is still part of the IT sales funnel and worth targeting.

Hopefully, this example has got you thinking about other services that are closely related to your offerings and connected in some way.

Server and Cloud Infrastructure Solutions Category

I have again included less apparent keywords in this category. Searches like

"server upgrade company + location."

"server to cloud company + location."

These are both highly relevant to most MSPs, but more than likely have little competition in your area in the search results.

Why has the competition missed them? It's due to the terminology of the search phrase. You will have a lot of MSPs targeting searches like:

"Office 365 migration services."

An excellent keyword to rank for but in reality is your potential client using the word "migration" in their search? This is IT lingo, but not what the average user (John Smith) is going to have in their vocabulary.

Again, this should hopefully provoke you down the thought process of that customer avatar. Our John Smith avatar is now forming in our head.

Office Manager and Policies Category

The final category is somewhat outside of John Smith's office door. John's the CEO but Anna is the office manager, and she needs help.

Tasked with managing IT supplier, and everything else that comes under office manager duties, she does not have a lot of time and is searching for quick wins. This includes having to come up with things like:

    The IT Budget
    The IT Policy for the company
    Internet Usage policy

And a raft of other such IT management tasks.

If you can help Anna out with free downloadable templates that are optimized for local search, you can not only save Anna's day but capture her contact details for a sales follow up.

The keyword list I have provided on the resources page may be somewhat overwhelming. Especially if you are thinking, how can you possibly come up with 100+ pages of content that are well written on your website.

We will get stuck into the prioritization in the content strategy, but I am going to leave you with this:

> Any time you publish something on the internet, it stays there for a very long time. Whilst you might only have one search for a "water leak detection system for a server room." You can quite easily be at the top position locally for such a search and expose your business to another potential client maybe not in 6 months from now, perhaps not in a year but sometime in the future the time invested today will pay off.

Checklist For Chapter 2
- Find out what the most profitable service is that you offer a quickest to perform.
- Research topics and keywords related to this service.
- Sketch out the sales funnel and ask 5 clients what they'd search if looking for this service.
- Collate your research as topics that form your content.

Chapter 3: Content Strategy & Planning

If you are like me you love technical detail. However, when it comes to conveying it to everyday use, things can get awkward very quickly.

One of the hardest tasks I had when learning how to optimize my site for search and market online was staying focused.

Over the course of the last ten years, I've come up with a winning formula that will help you produce content effortlessly for your website, and make your website visitors come back for more.

We're going to be delving deep into content strategy and how (with 1% more effort), you'll have a winning combination of engaging content that not only your visitors will love, but that Google will reward you for as well.

Why are you creating content?

This question hits home with me. Some IT firms pump out blog posts as they've been told that it's the right thing to do. But what exactly are the goals of having genuinely engaging content on your website?

Here's what I see are the two main reasons why you are producing regular content for your IT website:

1) Becoming an authority on IT by educating visitors to your site about IT, technology, and how it relates to their business.

You'll hear a lot of people in the MSP marketing space talk about educating your audience/users. The main reason for this is the fact that we are in the B2B market and education helps to build authority.

Becoming a trusted advisor and authority IT & technology give your potential clients the correct frame of reference about your company.

There's no better way to do this that providing valuable, useful content that your online audience (and potentially qualified leads) can take action on and use.

Remember Anna, the office manager that required that IT policy template.

While she's not going to sign a contract for a managed service agreement because you've provided her with an IT policy template on your website, you will be in her mind as an authority on the topic with regards to IT. All because you provided useful content which she could use.

What does this do for you immediately? Probably nothing. But it's all about stacking the value. Six months from now when you might be up to tender when their IT contract is up for renewal - you're going to have a much better chance of winning that business. Not only because you helped Anna out but also because you managed to capture Anna's details and follow up and ask the question "when's your IT contract due for renewal" using the lead magnet method.

If you can get into the mindset of creating useful content for your online audience Google will reward you naturally in the search results. That's the key strategy to having great content in the MSP space.

2) Adding value to your existing customer base

The secondary reason for generating content is to add value to your existing customer base. Not only are you going to publish all these impressive content pieces on your website for the benefit of SEO and share on your social channels for traffic and likes.

You can also include a summary of the content in an email newsletter to your existing customer base which is sent out on a monthly schedule. Then link the summary back to the original content on your webpage for some traffic signals that Google is watching for.

So, to recap - the goal of content on our website is:

To educate your online audience. This increases your authority, and you to use the lead magnet method to generate leads for your sales pipeline.

Secondary you can add value toy our existing client base by providing a monthly newsletter linking to your website content.

The output of this strategy will not only build your authority and educate your customers, but also as a side effect, Google will reward you if your content is engaging (more on engagement later).

That's the strategy in a nutshell, but where do you start? You've got six categories with over 100 keywords. How do you prioritize?

The answer is simple and something that I learned in my years of IT sales.

The Sales Matrix

"This is your last chance. After this, there is no turning back. You take the blue pill - the story ends, you wake up in your bed and believe whatever you want to believe. You take the red pill - you stay in Wonderland, and I show you how deep the rabbit-hole goes." Morpheus, The Matrix.

We all know what Neo did.

"I'm new to sales and don't have a clue what to do." These words were in my head for many months as I transitioned from senior systems engineer to IT sales. I could tell you how to roll back a Citrix hotfix but had a hard time picking up the phone and attempting to cold call.

This was until a sales improvement consultant came into the office one day and asked me the question, "what do you think is the easiest thing is to sell and who to?"

I looked blankly and had no idea. The response, "A service or product your existing client needs."

This hit me like a ton of bricks. Sell services to our existing client base - it's a lot easier to sell to someone that knows you than to a stranger.

The consultant then told me to write out all the monthly services that we offer, at the time this included the following:

- Managed services (IT Support)
- Backup services
- Website hosting services
- Antivirus protection
- Phishing Protection
- Business grade internet (leased lines here in the UK)

1. As an exercise, take this list and add them as columns to an excel spreadsheet.
2. On the right-hand side of the spreadsheet list all of your clients as a separate row.
3. Then with a bit of conditional formatting in excel put an X where that customer already has the associated service.

After a bit, you should have something like this:

Services	Managed Support	Backup Services	AV Protection	Phising Protection	Conectivity
Customer 1	x				x
Customer 2	x	x			x
Customer 3	x	x			
Customer 4			x		
Customer 5		x		✚	x
Customer 6	x	x			
Customer 7		x			x
Customer 8	x	x	x		x
Customer 9	x				
Customer 10		x			x

From this spreadsheet (aka, sales matrix) you will have a clearer picture of where there are opportunities in your existing client base.

These opportunities form the basis of your content prioritization.

You produce content around each of these services that educate your customer. This should be something timely associated with the service.

The reason you want something timely is that it will be a topic of conversation in your next "account management meeting."

For example, Anna's company is now on board with you, but they've been hesitant about your hosted VOIP solution for some months now. So, you bang out a great piece of content about how to secure their old style phone system/PBX. In the content, you educate your userbase about PBX fraud and steps to take to secure their old PBX. Near the end of the article, we talk about all of the benefits of a hosted VOIP solution as an alternative.

In preparation for tomorrow's account meeting with Anna send her a reminder with a link to your fresh piece of content.

Repeat this process for each of your existing clients that still require this solution.

Once you've discussed the usual topics of conversation and other points on the agenda at the account meetings, you then have an opportunity to discuss the PBX fraud subject.

The hook here is that you are in a great position to provide a quote on your hosted VOIP giving the reason that as an MSP you are dedicated to keeping that clients' business secure.

To recap:

Prioritise your website content by looking at what your existing clients need to be educated on.

This opens up opportunities to existing customers and helps prioritize the content calendar for the year.

Strategized Content Calendar

Various google ranking studies have been published over the last three years that point to long-form content as something that will help you rank for keywords you are targetting.

Studies suggest that the average pages in the top 10 google results are anything between 2000-2500 words (serpIQ study). With the average for position #1 being 1890 words (Semrush study).

Avg. Content Length of Top 10 Results

With that figure, you have to aim for blog posts (your website content) being at least 2000 words in length.

Take one look at your competitors, and I can bet the average is the 500-word count, if not less.

With that 2k figure in mind, you have to realistically ask, how regularly can you publish content on your website?

2000 words is not an easy number especially when you have to keep the reader engaged in the article.

In an ideal world, every fortnight would be a perfect amount of time to publish a new piece of content for your IT Business. However, you probably don't have enough time to sit down and write at such length on a regular basis. (Please note here that I mentioned you will have to write the content.)

This is something you can't outsource to Upwork, iWritter, WordAI or any other similar content writing service. The reason for this is that it has to be in your words. You will be connecting with your existing client base and potential new leads. The worst thing you can do is to have a piece of content written that does not align with your company culture, and more importantly, your professional opinion and expertise.

The content calendar is your roadmap for the next 12 months that will help you stay on track and execute the **bear attack** strategy.

Our topics will cover the following:

Educational opportunities - these are the blank holes you found in your service offerings to existing clients in the sales matrix.

Answers to common questions your customers ask - this is an easy one:

    1) Ask your engineers what are the most common problems they get

    2) Review your helpdesk for the last six months, do you see any recurring questions/problems that can form the basis of a content piece.

    3) Pick up the phone and ask your closest customers what they'd like to read about.

Timely and newsworthy - this would be recent IT stories that are hitting the news. For instance, at the time of writing (Jan 2018) Bitcoin has just hit an all-time high, Spectre meltdown was just announced.

All of these topics have a lot of questions that your clients, and others, want to know the answers to. Whilst the Spectre meltdown does somewhat align with your product/service offering. Bitcoin, on the other hand, relates to your business so you'll have to come up with an idea on how to spin this content piece to form a connection to your business, not just a relation. For example, advise your client that if they converted all the computers in your office to Bitcoin miners, here's how much money you'd produce in a year.

Seasonal articles:

December: IT year in review, round up of all IT related news.

July/August: How to keep your servers running cool in summer.

September: Back to school hardware.

November: Black Friday top 10 IT related products.

To recap - the content calendar will have the following strategic elements:

- Sales matrix opportunities
- Customer questions & answers
- Newsworthy
- Seasonal

Then, integrate our six keyword categories discussed in the last chapter.

IT Support
IT Security
DR and Backup
Network
Cloud & Server
IT Strategy and management

From this combination, you have the basis of what your content will look like for the next 12 months.

Chapter 2: Check list:
- Create the sales matrix.
- Prioritise your content based on the matrix.
- Create a content calendar to help you stay focused.

Chapter 4: Content Creation

I was truly awful at English in School. In fact, I still am. When I way in primary 5 (5th grade) I recall probably my darkest moment in childhood.

We were given a weekly spelling test. The teacher would read out a list of words, and we had to write out how we thought they were spelled in a small blue book. I suck at spelling, and this was way before spell check. The first few weeks I was bottom of the class. The teacher would tell me to look up the word in the dictionary.

This used to drive me mad as it's tough to find the correct spelling of a word in a dictionary if you don't know how the word is spelled in the first place. Not helpful at all.

As the weeks progressed, I got tired of having to read out my score in front of this whole class. Then it occurred to me - I could cheat.

The teacher in her wisdom made us mark our papers. When the correct spelling was read out, I would mark the wrong word as correct and total up my scores.

My luck had changed. I felt good about the fact that I'd outsmarted the teacher. This went on for months. Until parents night. My mum visited the teacher, and she reported on my progress. Included in this report was my spelling book which my mum proceeded to check over. She came back from parents night livid. I was so embarrassed.

I think I was around ten years old at the time and felt like hiding under a rock. Both teacher and mother were onto me. What I did not realize at the time was that my mum was not mad at me at all. She was angry at the teacher for cutting corners and allowing us to mark our books.

This experience showed me just how bad my spelling is. And, thanks to Spell Check, it hasn't improved much!. I'm lazy when it comes to looking at my errors and memorizing the correct spelling. With that childhood memory and lack of proper English education, content creation is something that I both hate and love.

I hate the thought of doing it - it's tough and a real challenge for me. To make matters worse writing about technology and products related to managed service in a language that everyone can understand is a task within itself.

However, if your content is excellent, you'll find that it will pay dividends for years to come.

You might be like me in some respects and wonder how the hell you are going to write content for your website. Ideally, you want articles of 1500 - 2000 words minimum. Writing 1500-2000 words is much easier said than done.

To help you, I've come up with a winning formula in structuring content, writing content and also appealing to the search engines.

First off, I use Grammarly plugin for Chrome. This is a free piece of software that will check your spelling and grammar. I like it better than MS Word as you can start typing straight from the browser and the way your errors are laid out on the page are clear.

The error checking within Grammarly is also a lot more accurate than MS Word.

The headline

First, you take the general idea of what you are going to cover. Turn that thought into an appealing click worthy headline. (Sometimes it seems I spend just as much time working on the headline for my articles as laying out the plan.)

Jon Morrow from Smartblogger has a high-quality PDF download called 52 Headline Hacks. This will get you off to a great start on how you should be formulating your headlines.

This, however, is only part of the headline equation. You've also got to come at it from what the search engines understand.

When formulating your headline make sure you keep in mind the intent of the article.

To give you an example:

If I wanted my article to promote our cyber security services, the headline would look like this: "Has your IT supplier provided you with cybersecurity awareness training?"

Your article would then go on to talk about the benefits of cybersecurity training to the business.

When would this article be found in the search? Well, it comes down to what you are answering in the headline and article.

Google is smart, brilliant.

Google analyses the intent behind your content and also the intent behind someone searching. Then matches both of these up.

The searcher has a question, Google then lists the best answers based on many factors.

Google will try and figure out what your content is about by using a variety of methods. These include the language used in your content.

It also measures how long someone will stay on the page and if they scroll down to read the article. Based on multiple tests it's able to categorize what answers your content provides the reader with.

The methods that Google employs has been carefully studied for years, and there's a lot of research - I'm not going to go into the detail here as it's a rabbit hole. Common sense applies.

Just remember – you are trying to give the best answer to a question someone is typing into Google.

How do you eat an elephant? One bite at a time. Chunk it down.

Once you have the headline figured out plan the content by chunking it down. As an example, for this chapter in the book I wrote down a list of what I wanted to cover:

- The story about my spelling at school
- Grammarly plugin
- Content headlines
- Chunking the content
- Engagement Rule
- APP Intro
- 80/20
- Localization

This forms the basis of a wire frame for the article. It also helps you stay linear, and because it's in a list format, it's much easier to get the article finished as you are not just making stuff up to fill 2000 words. You've got a clear plan of what you have to write about.

I already mentioned that Google measures how long a searcher stays on your content. This is sometimes called dwell time or engagement time. It's probably the number one SEO factor, and you need to know about this as it's crucial to the success of your content.

Your content has to be engaging, accessible to read, clear and you need to capture the searchers attention. You've got a very short window of time to do this.

Brian Deans from Backlink.io has an impressive technique called the <u>APP formula</u> which he starts out all of his articles with. The <u>APP formula</u> is all about gaining the attention of the website visitor. (APP = Agree, Promise, Preview.)

It's a short intro at the start of each article where you outline an idea, concept or problem that the searchers may have that you agree with. What this does immediately is show empathy (you understand their problem)

Agree Example:
I think you'll agree with me when I say it's tough to keep your staff educated on email phishing attacks. The problem is how you are going to solve it in the content.

Promise Example:
Well, it turns out if you have regular cyber security training you can dramatically reduce the risk of an email phishing attack.

And the preview is a golden nugget snippet of what there' going to read about.

Preview Example:
In the article, I'm going to outline what an email phishing attack looks like and the number one thing your staff need to know.

In this preview, I cheated a little as I opened a psychological loop - "the number 1 thing" the visitor now has to read on to find out what that number 1 thing is. I'll close the loop further down the page. Peppering these little loops in your content will work wonders for your content engagement.

Sell me this pen

One of the worst things you can do in your content is be overly sales focused this comes off as desperation.

The 2nd worst thing is not asking or reaching out in your content.

The general rule of thumb is that 80% of your content should be helping your reader. Useful information/educational that they can act on by themselves, now. If you can help the reader in the content, you have won 80% of the SEO battle.

Google knows when you have helpful content. That's why Google itself is such a handy tool - you go to it for answers and help - Google wants to give you the best results on every search. If Google came back with crap then you'd stop using it. Keep this in mind when you are producing your content.

The more you can educate your customers in your content the more you'll be seen as the authority on that content. This is the intended output of being helpful and educational in your content.

If you are the local IT authority online then when they need help they're going to think of you.

What about that 20%?

Reaching out or asking. How do you pull that off in your content? This is another well-known tactic of digital marketing. It's called the lead magnet. Its intended purpose is so that you can capture the reader's details and then reach out to them, ideally over the phone.

The lead magnet is generally some form of PDF download or access to specific content. Usually, a web form gives access to the magnet, and this is where you capture readers details.

Here's a list of some handy lead magnets to get you thinking:

- Downloadable Checklist - "10 steps to avoiding email phishing."
- Cheat Sheet - "8 Awesome Office 365 hacks."
- Template - "Password & Cyber Security Policy Template."
- IT Pro Toolkit - "Find out what tools the IT Pros use and why."
- Resource List - "Top 10 go to places for hardware & software."
- Spreadsheet - "Spend less on technology with this IT Budget spreadsheet."
- Form - "Get staff onboarding right with this new account user setup form."
- Guide - "How to double your internet speed without changing provider."

Localisation

Another item you have to take note of is localization of the content. This is almost getting into the realms of the technical SEO chapter, but I think it belongs here as your content must be localized.

What do I mean by localized? Well, most MSPs and IT companies operate in a local area. I know from experience that this is just the way it is for the majority of clients - they want local IT support.

Localising the content means including your location in the content. For example, if I were targeting IT security services, I would want to mention in the content what area(s) we operate in. There are so many local service companies that miss this step when they're producing content for their website. Having the location mentioned a few times in the blog post/article will work wonders for your rank.

Don't overdo it though. You only have to mention it once or twice since Google's Hummingbird algorithm knows when to show your site for local results, but it still helps to have the location mentioned for other search engines and when Hummingbird might not be picking your site up as it should.

The final word on content creation.

Imagine the blog post you are writing is going to be read by your dream customer. They are sick of their current IT provider and want to switch to someone that will get the job done correctly, and they're prepared to pay top dollar. They want to pay three months in advance to make the switch quicker.

This one blog post is your only chance. It's the first and last thing they are likely to read about your business. Every page on your website should have this frame of reference. More than likely if they are searching for a new IT provider they're only going to land on your website once. Your content needs to be rock solid: Build a habit, start writing.

Chapter Checklist
- Install Grammarly
- Download John Morrows headline PDF for ideas
- Practice the APP method
- Chunk down your article into sections
- Practice the APP method
- Remember to include localization keywords in your article

Chapter 5: Content Promotion

Have you ever written a blog post or video, spent countless hours perfecting it and then hitting the publish button only to find that no one reads your hard work? It's something I struggled with for years.

Planning and producing content is only half the battle. Content promotion is the next stage in kick-starting traffic to your website.

In this chapter, you'll learn what channels are available for promoting content.

I'll also dive I nto how you can use your existing customer base as the catalyst for search traffic to your website.

Scheduled Routine

Scheduling a routine and habit is required for content creation and promotion. Ideally, this should be a weekly task. Fortnightly or even monthly. 20 minutes is all you need.

If you were to actively use all the channels for promoting your content that would be a full-time job within itself. I highly recommend testing the water and identifying what channels work best for your business.

The first question is how to choose the right channel. Ask yourself where your audience is likely to hang-out online. It's all about your potential customer. Where are they online and will they engage in your content and find it interesting? Use that question to help steer the direction of your focus.

The 9 Channels

Social media

This book is not about best practices in social media marketing. We're going to use these platforms to help drive traffic to our content and website to help kickstart our online presence.

I won't be going into the intricacies of Instagram or any in-depth details on other social media platforms in particular - that's for the gurus.

What I will be covering are some of the possible avenues you can take to assist your website's online presence. Think of it like lighting a fire. You have to get the kindling before you can get the real heat. That initial spark of traffic from these channels add up over time, and when compounded, Google will take notice.

LinkedIn

Possibly the most appropriate social media channel for an MSP. I'd highly suggest using the article feature on LinkedIn. Write a concise piece about your topic and drop a link to your website content within the section. The whole purpose of the piece should be to direct the reader from LinkedIn to your website. Give them an incentive - open a physiological loop.

LinkedIn video and Youtube

Repurposing your written content in a 2-minute video will work wonders. I'd suggest the call to action at the end of your video is a "visit our website for the lead magnet". Mention the website address when talking, but don't link to it in the video description.

Why? The viewer will have to type your website address into their web browser manually. Believe it or not, this is a high ranking factor Google uses for SEO. It's known as direct traffic.

Twitter

I've gone off twitter, but it's a 10-second job to post a link to your article and make use of the relevant hashtags. Mention some industry experts, and you may even get a retweet.

Facebook

Repurpose the Youtube/LinkedIn video and upload a separate copy to facebook.

Don't link out to youtube or your content. Again only mention it in the directly uploaded video. Facebook's algorithm is designed to keep the user on Facebook so linking out will get your post seen by fewer people.

Facebook is useful when posting to relevant groups within the platform. Local groups, business network groups, and industry related groups. That's it. The less time spent there, the better - it's a time suck.

Auto-posting on social media

Don't use auto posters like Buffer etc. I've run experiments on social media channels in the past, and the engagement via auto posters drops off a cliff.

Reddit

You can gain a lot of traffic from Reddit, but the community on there will downvote your articles if it's just a blatant post to your website. You have to be helpful. There has to be a reason why you're posting a link to your website.

(I've heard going under a persona can work well on Reddit. This is where you don't appear to come across as the original content owner your but a third party that has a view on the associated content. Sneaky.)

Email

An email newsletter to your client base is a great way to keep communication channels open. Not only that, your existing clients are far easier to sell services and products to. Use this opportunity to link out to your new website content in the body of the newsletter.

Mail

Similar to email newsletters but in an offline format. I've not tried it yet, but you might even want to try mailing local businesses a hardcopy of your newsletter (that are not already your customers). I'm guessing it would have the opposite effect that email spam has. They'd probably be happy to receive it if you can stick to a monthly schedule.

Blog Comments

If you can find relevant blog articles on the web that are related to your article then drop a link in the comments section. The link to your content has to make sense and be helpful in the comments section. Don't just go blatantly linking to your content for the hell of it. You are being tracked by the rank brain, (Google's AI)!

For example, let's say I'd just written a piece on how to make your staff more efficient in Office 365.

I could perform a web search for: Office 365 tricks "no comments". This search is looking for relevant websites about office 365 and using the quotation brackets "no comments" I'm actively searching for blog posts with no comments.

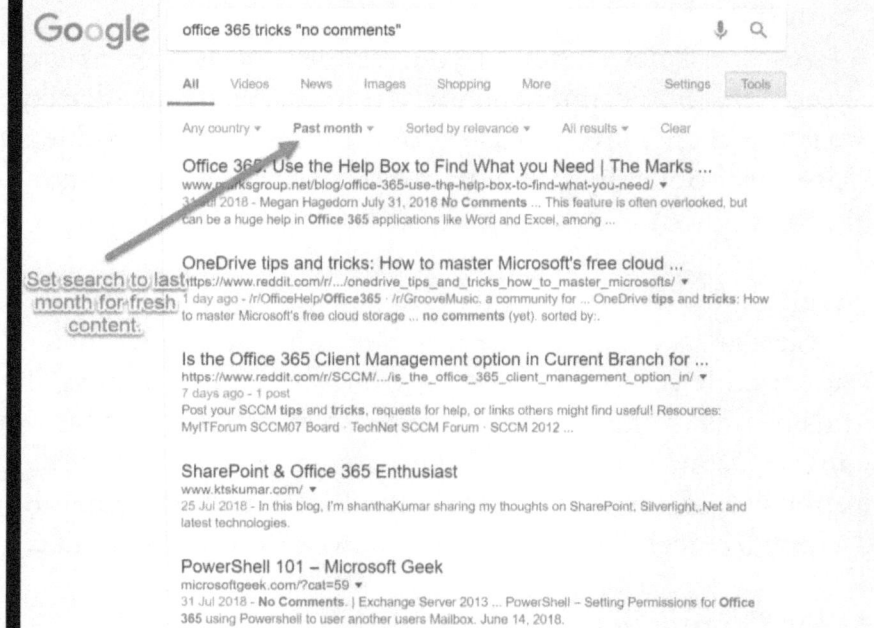

It's then just a case of crafting a unique, useful comment. Such as,

"Great article, I particularly liked tip number 6 - how to share files with using OneDrive. This has replaced our dropbox. I found some more useful tips here: http://linktomywebsite.com."

This comment not only compliments the original author, but also is on topic. The chances that your comment will be published after moderation are significantly higher.

Also note that once your comment is past moderation and posted most content management systems (like WordPress) will allow you to comment without going into the moderation queue. Good feature to know about for larger sites, but don't abuse it. Use it wisely and always keep a log of where you're leaving comments so you can check further down the line what got through moderation.

Buzzsumo can also help you in your task of finding favorite content where you can drop your comments. It's a search based tool that ranks content on how many times it has been shared across social platforms.

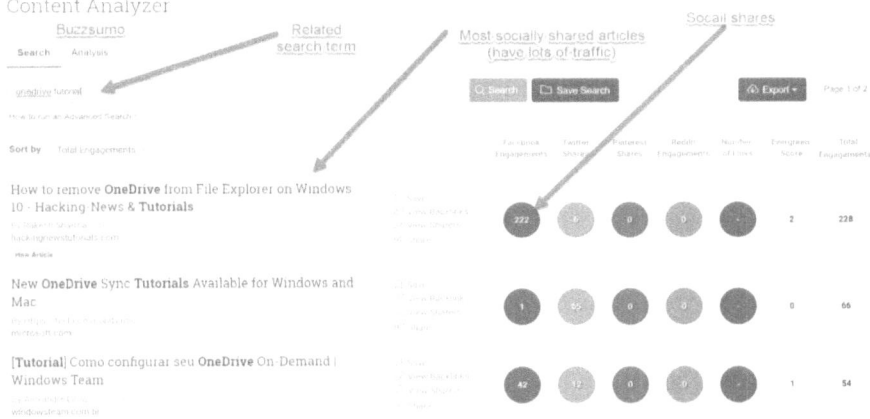

The more popular the content piece is that high it comes up in the search. The beauty of looking at popular content is that nine times out of 10 these pages will have a lot of search traffic already.

If you can craft a detailed comment with a link to your content, then you'll siphon off some of this traffic. The more engaging your content is, the more this siphon method will kick start your rankings in the search. Google will take note of your engagement, and your content will start to creep up the search results.

Quora

Quora is a place to share knowledge and to better understand the world. It has taken over from Yahoo Answers in the search, and with good reason. It's a place to post questions and where we helpful people (you and me) can post answers to questions.

Unlike Yahoo Answers, which is a little bit like the wild west), it is moderated by staff.

The right answers to questions rise to the top similar to Reddit.

There are 1000's of questions on Quora all looking for answers.

It's not 100% pure business on Quora so please keep this in mind if you are posing questions or answering questions.

Forums

I've used forums for 20+ years; but they seem to be on the decline due to social networks and Facebook groups. However, depending on where you live, you may have access to local business forums or just general local forums. These forums are a great place to share your knowledge ,experience, and links to your content.

If the forums allow, make sure you fill in all of your info on your profile with a link to your website. Some forums also let you include a signature line in your posts. This is a great place to mention your business name and what you do.

Business Networks (BNI, Chamber, etc.)

If you've ever been a member of BNI, you'll know all about asking for a specific referral every week. I've heard many times in my own BNI members ask the dreaded question "please share or like my Facebook page." I always cringe at the thought of members asking for this. I think the reason why I cringe is that if you're doing your job correctly in BNI and giving referrals, then you shouldn't have to ask for a like or a share.

What I would suggest is once you have an established relationship in BNI you ask permission to mention specific BNI members in your content, a post about a recent bit of business on which you've both collaborated. A result of this is that when you ask them to link to your content from their website/social account they'll be more than happy to and they'll love you for it.

Chamber of commerce

Here in the UK, all chambers have their own website and business news/blog section. This is the ideal place for you to do a small content piece that links to your more significant content piece on your website.

Some chambers are better than others, so it's worth asking what they'll help you do when promoting. I've seen chambers mention website articles directly in their email newsletter to members, while others will put up a blockade and limit what channels of theirs you can use. Investigation is key.

Your team

This is by far the most potent leverage you have available and must be done correctly.

No matter how small or how big your company is you can use your employee's social accounts to help promote your company's website content.

You do have to strike the balance right though. I'd highly suggest doing your research on your employee's social accounts, figure out who has the most followers or to put it another way who has the most influence?

With that fundamental fact ask that individual to help you produce a content piece and ask your team who'd be up for the challenge. This content piece could be something they are great at technically, something they could help you write, or just an idea for a topic to cover. The involvement they have is dependent on your company culture and existing relationship. Getting them on board at this stage will help you further down the line when it comes to publishing.

When the content piece is ready to promote, make it as easy as possible for your staff to share this across their channels. The fewer steps they have to go through the better, make it easy for them. If you have involved them in the content creation itself, then you'll have no problem at the promotion stage.

Final thoughts on content promotion.

I spoke to my wife about this topic in the book - I was finding it difficult on how to conclude the topic. When I told her the chapter was all about how to promote content for MSPs she just said - that's so boring - for businesses it's like choosing what toilet paper to use, who cares about IT.

As you can tell, she does not share the same passion as you or me about what we do as an MSP/IT business. It does take some energy and motivation, but I believe if you are passionate about what you do as a business and how you help others then you'll be excited about the possibilities laid out here.

My final thought on the matter is to be genuine and authentic in however you promote your content or business in general. What does your company stand for, why do you do what you do? I'm sure you've been asked that before. Carry that belief through to your content promotion methods.

Chapter Checklist:
- Find your content promotion channel
- Schedule content promotion as part of the overall process

Chapter 6: Lets get technical

When I first started out my SEO journey I didn't have a clue. Completely overwhelmed on where to start the engineer in me gravitated to the on-page technical side of SEO.

If you're just starting out in your SEO journey, it's safe to say prioritizing can be difficult and if you are anything like me, the technical side is appealing. With that in mind, it's worth stating that you can spend way too much time on the technical side.

I remember when I first started out I spent days setting up a slick PHP feed that would auto-populate my homepage. This was before I even knew about CMS's like WordPress and was coding manually. The hard work paid off, but to tell you the truth the on page technical side is only about 20% of the SEO battle now.

You will have the upper hand with site speed and an SSL certificate on your site, but a lot comes down to your on page content and how the user interacts with your website. I've put together what I believe to be the most important ranking factors in this chapter.

Large SEO related companies like MOZ, SEMrush and incredibly popular bloggers in the SEO space put out an annual "ranking factor" report. These reports form the basis of this chapter where we take a close look at the most important on-page SEO elements.

Just to be clear when I use the term "on page" I mean how your website pages are structured.

A word of warning - don't get stuck in detail here - spend too much time on the technical side and your content will suffer. Strike a balance.

The Landscape has changed. Back when I first started out in SEO there was a focus on populating your content with target keywords, including these keywords in places like your meta description, headings and there's even a meta keyword tag which almost every SEO worth their salt used on a daily basis.

These on-page elements would make huge improvements in your search position for a given keyword. But just like everything - people gamed the system and took advantage of these easy wins.

Google caught on, as did other search engines like Bing, and now you have to be careful not to over optimize your pages as this will have the opposite effect. When it comes to crafting your on-page SEO it's now all about being natural, helpful and having the user experience at the top of your mind.

Site Speed (host, page render, image compression)

Over the years site speed has been something that not many cared about in the SEO industry,y but it's now a crucial part of your website strategy. This really comes down to the user experience. There's nothing worse than browsing a website that has a really slow page load, or worse the page just does not seem to load at all. This leaves you second guessing if it's the device youarre browsing on, your internet or something else.

Sites like Facebook and Amazon are well aware of just how important it is to have a fast responsive website that loads the first time, every time, and is never down. Heck Amazon's AWS came about due to their demand for 100% uptime.

When was the last time you went to Facebook and had a bad experience with pages not loading? I can count on one hand in the last 10 years of daily Facebook browsing that I've had page load issues.

You should be aiming for 100% uptime and fast page and server speed for your business's website. Google will mark your website down the ranking if it has a slow response time. The search giant started paying close attention to site speed back in 2014 when it was obvious just how much mobile traffic has exploded on the web.

There are a few tools to measure your website speed. Google will even tell you how your website scores out of 100%. You can find links to these tools in our resources section: https://www.itrockstars.co.uk/resources

The tools themselves will even let you know why your pages might not be loading as fast as they could. The two main factors that I see in the MSP space:

1) Bad wordpress themes that require optimized - there are many page speed experts that will tweak the code behind your CMS & theme to make it load much faster.

2) Website host. This is something you probably didn't think of when you first launched your website. If you got a website company to do the work now, they'd be aware of how important the host is. But a few years ago it was not a big deal.

I personally use WP Engine. This is because I work in WordPress and their hosting is basically an uber-optimized version of a WordPress install running on some slick SSD based servers. There are many hosts to choose from and it's worth paying a premium for fast hosting.

SSL

Who would have thought having an SSL certificate installed on your site would be a ranking factor? I always assumed SSL certificates were only something you required on a website if you were processing sensitive customer information or in financial services. Google has made it a much more important ranking factor in recent years. Their push for a more secure web has almost every web agency in the know launching sites that are SSL enabled.

From an MSP perspective, it's really practice what you preach. With such a heavy focus on cybersecurity, your company should be leading the way in having an SSL certificate on your website. It's a no-brainer.

Title tag

The title tag on your website pages is the first thing someone will see when they are searching.

It's your first and last opportunity to draw in the user and make them click on your web result in the search. You have approximately a 50-60 character limit to play within the title tag.

The Most Common Types of Cyber Security Attacks | Rapid7 ⬅ Title Tag
https://www.rapid7.com/fundamentals/types-of-attacks/ ▾
What are the most common **cyber security** attacks being performed today? Let us tell you about them.
Learn more.
SQL Injection Attacks (SQLi) · Phishing Attacks · Malware Attacks · (MITM) Attacks

Cybersecurity Threats - Center for Internet Security ⬅ Title Tag
https://www.cisecurity.org/cybersecurity-threats/ ▾
The CIS and MS-ISAC® **cybersecurity** professionals analyze **risks** and alert members to current online **security threats**. ... Critical Patches Issued for Microsoft Products, August 14, 2018 MS-ISAC ADVISORY NUMBER: 2018-091 DATE(S) ISSUED: 08/14/2018 OVERVIEW: Multiple vulnerabilities ...

10 Cyber Security Threats In 2017 | Purple Griffon ⬅ Title Tag
https://purplegriffon.com/blog/10-cyber-security-threats-in-2017 ▾
23 Mar 2018 - How can we be expected to keep up to date with all the potential **Cyber Security threats** that are emerging? It's becoming increasingly difficult to ...

What is cyber security? – IT Governance ⬅ Title Tag
https://www.itgovernance.co.uk/what-is-cybersecurity ▾
Cyber security comprises technologies, processes and controls that are designed to protect systems, networks and data from **cyber** attacks. Effective **cyber security** reduces the risk of **cyber** attacks, and protects organisations and individuals from the unauthorised exploitation of systems, networks and technologies.

Title tag fusion

This is what I now call my method when creating a title tag. It's a combination of my target keyword, what the page is about wrapped into an appealing click bate wording.

Here's an example:

My target keyword is "Office 365 productivity"

My page is a guide on some of the most efficient features of Office 365.

My title tag looks like this: *5 Office 365 productivity hacks will change the way you work*

It's very similar to writing a headline for a post but including your target keyword and describing what the page is about. No mean feat. Especially as you are limited to 60 characters maximum (including spaces). It will take some time to get this right, but once you do it becomes a lot of fun.

It's worth noting, that you don't always have to use your target keyword in the title tag. Whilst this was key back in the early SEO days Google understands the intent of your title. So if you are scratching your head when fusing your title keep this in mind.

Description

Whilst the meta description (the bit under the title tag in search results) does not impact ranking factors directly, it is associated with page click-through rate.

Cutover migration to Office 365 - Office 365
https://support.office.com/.../cutover-migration-to-office-365-9496e93c-1e59-41a8-9... ▼
In a cutover migration, on-premises mailboxes are migrated to Office 365 in a single migration batch.
In the Exchange admin center, go to Recipients > Migration. Choose New > Migrate to Exchange
Online. On the Select a migration type page, choose Cutover migration > next.

How to Migrate to Office 365 - dummies
https://www.dummies.com/software/...office/office-web.../how-to-migrate-to-office-3... ▼
How to Migrate to Office 365. You begin the process of adding a user by selecting the New ·User
button from the Ribbon of the Users screen. Migrate mailbox data (Exchange) to Office 365. To begin a
new migration, click the New tab to begin walking through the Migration wizard.

Microsoft Office 365: Make a Smooth Move to the Cloud | TechNet ...
https://technet.microsoft.com/en-us/library/gg675925.aspx ▼
There are myriad factors to consider when migrating your users to the cloud, but the Microsoft Office
365 environment helps ease the path.

10 major Office 365 gotchas to avoid | Computerworld
https://www.computerworld.com/.../office.../10-major-office-365-gotchas-to-avoid.ht... ▼
22 Sep 2014 - From unrealistic design decisions to costly add-ons, the migration path to Microsoft
Office 365 is fraught with hidden pitfalls.

Meta Description

How to migrate from Exchange 2010 to Office 365 - step by step guide
https://www.codetwo.com/admins-blog/migrate-exchange-2010-office-365/ ▼
30 Jan 2018 - Exchange 2010 to Office 365 Migration is a complex process. This article lists and
describes the available native migration options. The ...

Someone looking down a list of search results will quickly scan the meta description. This is your opportunity again to draw in the user with a precise and descriptive sentence or two about what's on the page. Here's an example for out Office 365 Productivity page:

> "Learn how to be more efficient using Office 365 using these top professional tips. Including; Outlook, Excel, Word, Teams & Flow"

In this example, I'm detailing what the article covers this not only informs the searcher but also the search engine as I'm using words which are closely related to Office 365 (Excel, Words, etc.).

When working in the description tag is you can use language that is closely related to your main topic this can help the search engines determine what your content is likely to be about.

URL slug

Just like the title and meta description, the URL slug (path to your page on your website) is present in the search results.

Google will pull out the keywords from the URL slug and highlight these also in the search. Another opportunity to increase the click-through rate from the search results to your website.

> **Windows Server Backup Solutions – Acronis Backup**
> https://www.acronis.com/en-gb/business/backup/windows-server/ ▼
> Back up Your Windows Server to Hybrid Cloud Storage and Recover Your Entire Server ... Acronis
> **Backup** is the world's easiest and fastest **backup solution** that ...
>
> **Best Server Backup Software | 2018 Reviews of the Most Popular ...**
> https://www.capterra.com/server-backup-software/ ▼
> Find and compare **Server Backup Software**. Free, interactive tool to quickly narrow your choices and
> contact multiple vendors.
>
> **Cloudwards Guide: The 9 Best Server Backup Solutions**
> https://www.cloudwards.net/best-server-backup-so utions/ ▼
> 29 Jun 2015 - Cloudwards Guide: The 9 Best **Server Backup Solutions**. IDrive Business. CloudBerry
> **Backup**. Carbonite for Office. Acronis **Backup** 12.5. StorageCraft. Macrium Reflect 7. NovaBACKUP.
> EaseUS Todo.
> IDrive Business · CloudBerry Backup · Acronis Backup 12.5 · StorageCraft
>
> **The Best Windows Server Backup 2018 - Cloudwards**
> https://www.cloudwards.net › Cloud Storage ▼
> 10 Apr 2017 - Today we're going to explore the options available to **backup** your **server** and review the
> best Windows **server backup solutions** of 2017. Why **Backup** Your **Server**? CloudBerry **Backup**.
> Acronis **Backup** 12. Storagecraft ShadowProtect SPX **Server**. Veritas Backup Exec. Datto Siris 3.
> Macrium Reflect 7.

(URL Slug)

I try to keep my URL paths uncomplicated and straightforward. From a user perspective this means that I don't include the category or any other structure in my slug; just the website address and page.

For example: www.itrockstars.co.uk/blog/cloud-computing/some-great-office365 productivity-tips/

This is the wrong way to do it. There's no reason to categorize my site structure in this way. If I were running a large e-commerce website with 1000's of products, then that would make sense for both web bots and the user. However, for a local IT business that's posting maybe once a week at most then it's not required.

Also, there's is really no reason to have the words "some & great" in the slug. Leave the descriptive words for the title and meta description.

As already mentioned, Google highlights the keywords so stick to a structure of 3-4 words with no stop words (I, a, about, an, are, as, at, be, by, in, is, it, of, on, or, that, the, this, to, was, what, when, where, who, will, with, the.)

Here's the right way - simple, clear, concise: www.itrockstars.co.uk/office365-productivty-tips

From this example, you can see I've used my exact target keyword.

Content (size, readability)

The general rule of thumb is to keep your articles to a word count of 1500-2500 words. It's been proven that longer articles rank higher in the search.

A lot of this comes down to the user experience and interaction of your content and page itself. If you've got pop-ups or banner ads, this can distract from the content itself. You need to draw the reader in, so the fewer distractions, the better.

Don't forget what your page looks like on a mobile. I tend to use a large font for my content. From a mobile perspective, this tends to work well as the user does not need to pinch and zoom on their screen to read my content.

Outbound Links

Outbound links were always thought to be a ranking factor. Guidance from Google on this topic suggests that you should only link out from your website when it makes sense in the content.

Example: "Microsoft's Office 365 has changed the way businesses operate with their IT systems."

Does linking to Microsoft in this sentence make sense? Not really. Everyone knows who Microsoft are and linking to the home page of MS's site is not going to help the user that's come to our website to read up about Office 365 productivity tips.

Here's the correct way to link in your content:

"There are many apps in the Office 365 suite here's a list of them all. In this article, we're going to cover the most popular."

Linking to a list of the apps and what they do is probably of use to the reader. They've come to your site looking for productivity tips. If they gotten a better perspective of the Office365 suite, this is going to help them in their quest.

Images

Images and gifs can make your page come alive. They not only help the user to interact with your pages, but they can also help split up walls of text.

One feature of embedding images on your website that can help search engines understand what your page is about is the image alt tag. This is text embedded in the HTML with an alternate text specified, usually used if for some reason images are disabled on the browser, slow connection speed or for the blind.

It's also an opportunity for us to tell the search engines what the image is.

Use descriptive text for the image alt tag. Wordpress and other CMS's allow you to quickly enter alt text when inserting the image in the content of a post. Whatever you do, don't start stuffing your keywords in here. That's an old trick that Google does not like.

Other data metadata that can be useful for the search engines associated with images is the geolocation information attributed to the image. This data is automatically embedded in most smartphone photos and high-end DSLR cameras where location services are turned on.

You may have an image to hand that represents something local to your area from stock or similar with no geolocation data. In such instances it's useful to embed the geolocation data, this is something that can be done with various online tools. Check the resources page for more information. See https://www.itrockstars.co.uk/resources

Final image optimization technique that can have a significant impact on search ranking is the compression of your images on the page. This comes back to page speed load time. Make sure your images are compressed and sized correctly for the page. (I make this one of the first tasks when doing a site audit.)

Load all the images up in FTP and run through a compression tool then re-upload. It's quickly done and can cut down drastically on the page load time of your website.

Chapter checklist:

- Choose a fast website host and optimize your website for fast load times.
- Install an SSL cert if you haven't
- Keep URL slugs simple
- Optimise title and description meta tags for click through rate in the search results.
- Keep in mind what's best for the user when they arrive at your website.

Chapter 7: What not to do

As mentioned at the beginning of this book, I have made a lot of mistakes when it comes to SEO. The moral of the following story is simple. <u>Think long term about your business.</u>

I'm not proud of the following story, in fact, I'm a little ashamed that I got involved in such a sleazy business.

The year was 2012, I'd been optimizing local business websites for about 4 years. I was a the top of my local SEO game and had three separate businesses with a team of people running all thanks to the ability I had to rank local websites on the first page of the search engines.

I was burnt out and looking for a way out. In my search for a way out, there was one online forum that I always kept coming back to, Wickedfire. At the time the community was thriving and was made up of SEO pros, affiliates and people looking to make a quick buck.

I was in the latter category. I'd heard about all the riches that could be accumulated in affiliate marketing, which is funnelling traffic to a product or service and taking a cut of commission for each sale.

At the time here in the UK, the payday loan market was starting to heat up, and there were some prominent newcomers to the online payday loan scene. I'd caught word of this via some private messages on Wickedfire.

I quickly set into action my first attempt at affiliate marketing. I purchased a domain, put some basic content up then headed over to Wickedfire services where you could buy spam linking packages.

Google back then was very easy to game/ All that was required was many backlinks from other websites. The spam package I purchased was called Spamwow from memory. It was probably the best $100 investment I ever made.

Three days after purchasing the spam links package, my website started to rise in the search very quickly. I was targeting a particular keyword "XXXX promo code", where XXXX was the name of the payday loan company. Due to legal reasons, I am not going to mention the actual company here as that would just be asking for more trouble.

Anyway, there's a massive amount of money to be made in targeting the word "promo code," "voucher code, "coupon code" appended with a well-known service or product. If someone is buying online, there's a good chance they'll search for a code before they buy. Usually, this happens when the company in question has a promo code field in their order form. Well, the payday loan company in question had one, and they were advertising heavily on the TV and radio here in the UK. This meant that there were around 5000 people every day searching for this particular keyword.

After two weeks I hit number one in the Google search for this term. I had a promo code on the front page of my website and an affiliate link to the loan provider. Commission was £25/$35 for every successful transaction I sent to the loan provider.

I would get an email every time a commission was made. I remember the very first payment. I was out walking in the hills of Aberdeenshire, about 30 minutes from where I live up a hill range called Bennachie. I was full of energy and about halfway up the 500m range when the first email came through. What I'd been reading on Wickedfire about the riches to be made in affiliate marketing seemed to become a reality. By the time I reached the top of Bennachie, I had received five more emails. I'd always been driven by money and was ecstatic with what was happening. Most people would not admit to this, but I'm laying it all out here.

Over the course of the next few weeks, I was regularly checking my email and planning what I was going to do with my new found fortune. The first thing I did was pay off my student loan. This always seemed like a massive chain around my neck, a tax here in the UK that's taken directly off your salary.

The second course of action was to plan out how I was going to sustain this income. I knew it was going to be short lived.

In my stupidity, I went and purchased an almost new BMW convertible. The z4, commonly known as a "hairdressers" car. My wife loved it, but I found the thing too low to the and the and bonnet stuck out a mile. That added with the white leather seats made it probably the stupidest purchase of my lifetime.

Two weeks into my new fortunes and things took a dramatic turn of events. I received a big white envelope in the mail. Documentation of some sort. As I opened it, I knew it was not good going to be good.

The letter was from a legal firm based in London. On behalf of their client (the payday loan company I'd been sending lots of traffic to), had issued a cease and desist on my promo code website. I could not understand exactly how or why they did this, but after some research, I quickly learned that the domain name I purchased infringed on the payday loans trademarked company name.

The emotion I was feeling at the time was one with worry. I had no legal protection, and the entire operation was under my name, not a limited company or LLC. In theory, I could lose everything if this went any further. I had no choice. I had to hand over the domain name to the loan provider. I was scrambling to come up with a plan to keep my website at the top of the search. Having just taken on the new car I was up a creek.

There was only one thing for it - start a brand new fresh website that does not infringe on any trademarks. I set to work. However, things did not improve. The year 2012 saw the release of Google's Penguin algorithm.

At the time this algorithm was programmed to identify websites with spam backlinks. My site was on Google's radar. The algorithm has gotten a lot smarter since 2012, but at the time it was looking for websites with an unusual ration of keywords in the backlinks.

For example If I start building links to my website from other websites and make the anchor word "IT Support" and use the same keyword many times as backlink text, in a way which is not natural, the Penguin algorithm will detect the unusual pattern and knock my website back down the google search.

When the algorithm was first launched many online businesses ceased trading overnight. Their business operation had been built on too many backlinks. After a few months of this new algorithm being live things took on an even worse turn. Professional SEO'ers managed to figure out exactly what had changed and what the algorithm did. These players soon evolved. How? Negative SEO.

Sending your competitor a stack of backlinks with the same anchor text - this in the eyes of google looked like you were trying to game the system but what was happening was that your competitor was attempting to knock your site from its position.

The payday loan niche I was operating in at the time just became a flame war with everyone applying this negative SEO tactic. The writing was on the wall as soon as I saw my site get taken down. It was time to bail.

I went into an SEO hibernation period for over four years. Since then the SEO industry has matured. Search engines, in general, are a lot smarter. Google has released many new algorithms including Rank Brain which makes it very difficult to game the system.

What can be learned from this tale?

- Don't buy links.
- Don't try and game the system.
- Be strategic and plan for the long-term goals for your business.
- Build strong foundations for your website.
- Watch out for trademarks in your content and website.
- Incorporate your company, so you have legal protection.

Chapter 8: Hacking the Map pack

One of the easiest wins in SEO is optimizing your business listing in the search.

It's also one of the best ways to obtain a significant amount of traffic.

Both Goole and Bing offer the ability to submit your business listing to their services. If you have not already done this you may still have a listing.

Many businesses are not aware that you can manually submit or claim your businesses listing, it's the first step to optimizing your position in what I call the "map pack".

Google map pack example:

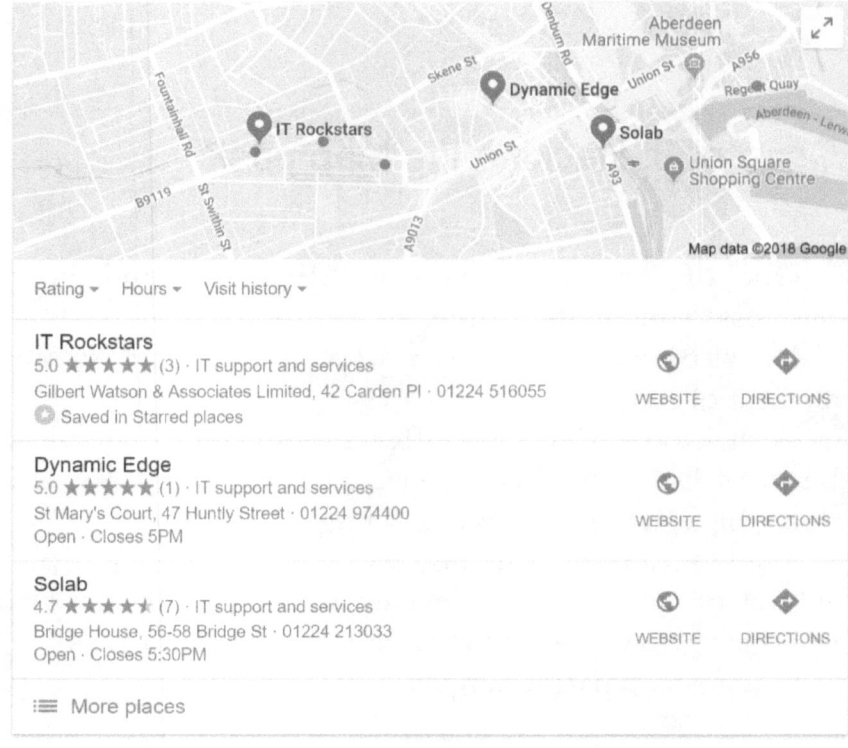

Just like your website, there are ranking factors involved on-page (the listing) and off-page (citations). We're going to cover both ranking factors and also include a little-known tip that will guarantee your place in one of the top positions.

Google My Business Listing

The Google Business Listing is really what this whole chapter is about. Yes, Bing offers a similar service, and yes you should be listing your business with Bing (because it's not Google) too as it will account for some traffic.

Follow the process prescribed for both. If you've not claimed your business listing do it now.

Yorokobi by CJ

Website   Directions   Save

4.5 ★★★★⯪ 149 Google reviews
Japanese restaurant

Restaurant with bay windows, dado panelling and a corner bar, serving Japanese and Korean cuisine.
Address: 51 Huntly St, Aberdeen AB10 1TH
Your past visits: You visited 1 year ago · Editing
Hours: Closed · Opens 5:30PM ▾
Phone: 01224 566002
Menu: yorokobibycj.co.uk

Suggest an edit · Own this business?

Claim your lisitng

Know this place? Answer quick questions

(Awesome place to go for Sushi if you ever visit Aberdeen!)

Best practices for your business listing should include as much information as possible. This means entering the following items at a minimum:

> Business name (Self Explanatory)
> Address (Your main office address)
> Landline telephone number (not mobile/cell)
> Business description (750 character limit)

Keep the customer in mind when writing the business description, don't over complicate with technology babble, this will confuse your potential client. Include in the description some of your main keywords but don't force them in, only use where it makes sense. Natural language showing empathy is vital.

Photos

This is your opportunity to include photos for your business description. I always include the company logo, photos of the team, inside the office and some technology related pictures. Ideally, these photos should be geocoded with longitude and latitude data appended. Check the resources page for a geocoding tool: https://www.itrockstars.co.uk/resources

Use file names that are descriptive of the photo. The more professional these photographs are the better.

Services

Here you can include your primary business activities. This comes down to what you want to be found for in the search. Focus in on your most profitable services in this area. There is also an option to include pricing along with the service description.

I'd highly suggest not to include any pricing in business listings or on your website. Potential customers would love to see this information up front however it's not the time nor the place to be making this information publicly available.

You have to be speaking with them in person to explain the value of your services - this is an offline process and not something you should be doing on your website.

Categories

If you are being outranked in the map pack by competitors locally, I suggest looking at their categories. The only issue with this is that you can see only the primary category they're listed for.

Google my business allows many categories.

There's a little-known hack that allows you to see all of your competitor's categories.

Simply go to your competitor's map view and look up the page source in Chrome.

Ctrl+F their main category – in this example we are looking for "IT Support and services"

```
[,null,null,null,null,null,null,null,null,1,1]\n,[null,null,null,null,null,[[[[0,0]\n,[458,768]\n],[[974,0]\n,[1024,768]\n]\n,
ll,null,null,null,null,null,null,[null,null,1]\n]\n","])}'\n[[null,[[null,null,null,n@ther-categories1,\"@5p3W-qiJ-HHgAaq-
ll,null,[\"@5p3W-qiJ-HHgAaq-bGIAQ\",\"@ahUKEwiqz_XI8fTcAhXhI8AKHap8DBEQ8BcIAygAMAA\", \"47 Huntly
ll,null,[\"http://www.google.co.uk/search?
4B10+17r\\u00261udocid\\u003d724412748729049723941rd\\u003d0x488411d9615fc3f7:0x64884f9/9397d8d7,1\\\"1
null,null,null,5.0,1]\n,null,null,
,AOvVaw2_VfeHhwov6XErR_ebqw_K,,@ahUKEwiqz_XI8fTcAhXhI8AKHap8DB8EQO61gIDig3MAA,,\"]\n,null,
Dx64884f919397d8d7\",\"Dynamic Edge\",null,[\"IT support and services\",\"Computer Consultant\",\"Telecommunications Service
47 Huntly Street, Aberdeen AB10 1TH\",null,null,null,null,[[[[2,null,null,null,null,[null,null,null,1,0]\n,
ll,0,17 \n]\n]\n]\n,[null,null,null,null,null,null,null,null,[null,1519205316151,null,1519207233867,[[2018,1,21]\n,
7,2]\n,[2016,7,2]\n]\n]\n,[null,1469803348336,null,1469808589929,[[2016,6,29]\n,[2016,6,29]\n]\n]\n,
1]\n]\n [null,1469704725235,null,1469721968974,[[2016,6,28]\n,[2016,6,28]\n]\n]\n,[null,1469539124504,null,1469542879909,[[2016,6,26]
6,25]\n [2016,6,25]\n]\n,[null,1469431875400,null,1469444599787,[[2016,6,25]\n,[2016,6,25]\n]\n]\n,
1]\n]\n [null,1469086602769,null,1469095035496,[[2016,6,21]\n,[2016,6,21]\n]\n]\n,[null,1468826655534,null,1468839454946,[[2016,6,18]
6,15]\n,[2016,6,15]\n]\n]\n,[null,1468500844000,null,1468512354997,[[2016,6,14]\n,[2016,6,14]\n]\n]\n,
```

Under the primary category in the page source, you'll see all their other categories. (Computer Consultant, Telecommunications Services in the image above.)

If you are smart what you'll do is go one step further than this. Create a big spreadsheet with 10 large cities and your main keywords. Look at the primary and secondary category for the highest-ranking map packs in the largest cities. You'll be able to spot the trends on what categories to choose for your target keywords.

Citations

Citations are ranking factor in your business listing. I class this as off page, similar to link building on other websites. However, where it differs from link building is that the number of citations you have will improve the likelihood your business listing will rank higher in the search. (For info, a citation is a reference to your business in the form of a NAP.)

Name, address and phone number.

Building citations is tedious. However, it's something that has to be done correctly, don't outsource this to a 3rd party. If you misspell a word, change the format of your address or format of your phone number between citations they'll be inconsistent and can affect ranking.

The 2nd rule is to keep track of login details the URL, email address and password you use when creating accounts for all of the citations. The main reason for this is if you change address anytime in the future, or spot inconsistencies in your citations, which can easily happen when you're working through the list.

Then it's just a case of referring to your account spreadsheet to log in and change where there's an error or significant update.

That brings us onto the list of citations. Where can we go and get citations?

There are some public sites where you can be building citations. These are the top tier citation sources both Google and Bing use to create their database:

- Acxiom

- Apple Maps
- Bing
- CityGrid
- Facebook
- Factual
- Foursquare
- Infogroup/ExpressUpdate
- Localeze
- Superpages
- Yahoo!
- YP
- Yelp

This list is the top citation sources for Google USA. Please refer to the resource page for other countries at https://www.itrockstars.co.uk/resources

This list is a good place to start when building citations. Make sure when entering company description of each of these sources that you change up the text.

This helps avoid duplicate detection penalties from Google and gives your citations more of a chance of ranking in the search than otherwise would be the case if all the citations were exactly the same. Just keep in mind the NAP should remain consistent.

The final citation step is finding other sources, this can be an ongoing task as lower tiered directories are always changing. To find other citations look at where your competitors have citations. The easiest way to do this is an exact match search in Google using their phone number.

[Screenshot of Google search results for "01224 516181" showing about 8 results including TheTechForce Ltd, Chapter Members - BNI, Facebook listings, shouldianswer.co.uk, and Aberdeen & Grampian Chamber of Commerce.]

Also, make sure to use variant formats of the phone numbers and go through the top ranking competitors in the map pack.

This process can be made much easier using a tool called White Spark that will actively monitor your citation sources and your competitor's citation sources. There's a small fee for this tool but well worth the investment for a return in the top three places in the map pack.

Pay close attention to industry relevant citations and directories. For example, Microsoft has the partner pinpoint (partner) directory. IT Rockstars also have a directory https://www.itrockstars.co.uk/it-company-directory/ again you can find a list of industry relevant directories on the resources page.

Reviews

Another important ranking factor in the map pack is your reviews and rating. It's not an area that I used to concentrate on as having a 5-star review does not automatically equate to being in the top position in the map pack. However, it will increase the CTR (click through rate) to your website if you have positive insightful reviews about your business. Users are more likely to click through to your website.

The easiest way to get reviews from existing customers is to ask them.

Making this a simple process for your customer is something to take in mind. This can be done by generating a review link which you can include in an email when asking your customer base:

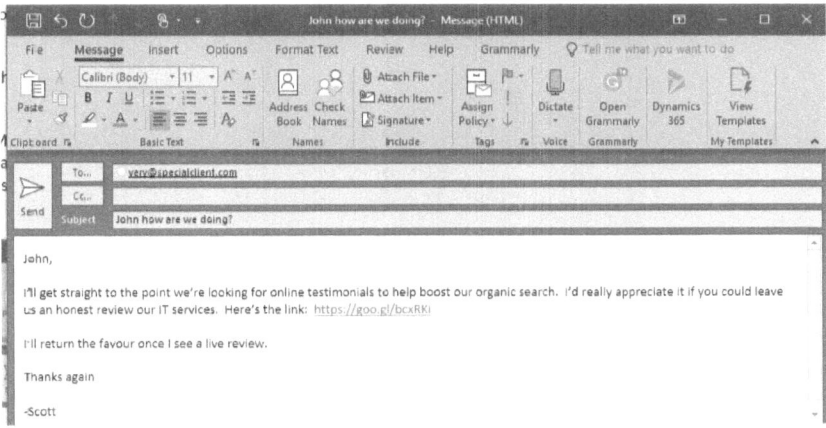

There are lots of different options on how you would go about asking your customers to leave a review, and timing is also important. Account management meetings are a good time to ask in person. Follow this up with a reminder email if they've not yet taken action

JSON Injection & Rich snippets

Rich snippets are structured data mark-up that you can include in your page's HTML. This helps search engines understand what your content is.

You've already seen this before if you've looked for a movie listing, the structured data is pulled direct from a website into the Google search:

Structured data appearing in the search.

Other examples of rich snippets are the review stars you see in the search.

Rich snippet example for "IT Support London"

There are many types of structured data for reference. The best place to see all the different types of mark-up available is on Schema.org which is a community that maintains schema structure for the internet.

For the purpose of an MSP/IT Business there are two main mark-ups we're interested in:

Local Business & Reviews

The local business mark-up tells Google and other search engines our website is a local business. The mark-up itself includes fields where you can enter your company's NAP.

Example of Local Business Microdata formatting:

```html
<div itemscope="" itemtype="http://schema.org/LocalBusiness">
    <span itemprop="name">Gene's Delicious Donuts</span><br>
    <link itemprop="url" href="http://www.example.com">
    <span itemprop="address" itemscope="" itemtype="http://schema.org/PostalAddress">
        <span itemprop="streetAddress">123 Happy Lane</span><br>
        <span itemprop="addressLocality">Irvine</span>, <span itemprop="addressRegion">CA</span>
        <span itemprop="postalCode">92618</span>
    </span><br>
    <a itemprop="telephone" href="tel:+15551112345">(555) 111-2345</a><br>
    <span itemprop="faxNumber">(555) 111-2345</span><br>
    <span itemprop="email">you@domain.com</span>
    <link itemprop="logo" href="image/path/file-name.jpg">I
    <link itemprop="sameAs" href="https://plus.google.com/your-google-url">
    <link itemprop="hasMap" href="https://www.google.com/maps/place/link-to-your-business">
    <span itemprop="geo" itemscope="" itemtype="http://schema.org/GeoCoordinates">
        <meta itemprop="latitude" content="111.00000">
        <meta itemprop="longitude" content="-96.012345">
    </span><br>
    <time itemprop="openingHours" datetime="Mo, Tu, We, Th, Fr 09:00-17:00">9 AM - 5PM</time>
</div>
```

Handy tip – you can get your business's longitude and latitude from Google maps listing.

The best way to include it on your page is using JSON-LD scripting language. This will make your page load faster and is easy to use compared to other methods.

The code itself once created for your business can then be injected into your site's HTML.

Google offers a structured data testing tool which can help with the task of creating the correct JSON mark-up with no syntax errors.

To make the task even easier, I've included a JSON/Structured data generator on the resources page https://www.itrockstars.co.uk/resources.

Enter your business information in and the JSON script will automatically be created.

Then it's just a simple case of copying this code and pasting into your website's HTML in the relevant pages.

Google does take rich snippet spam seriously so to respect this, and to avoid any ranking penalties, I include the JSON code on my homepage and location/contact page. These seem like the most obvious places that you'd add your location data for the search engines to use.

```
<script type="application/ld+json">
{
"@context": "http://schema.org",
"@type": "LocalBusiness",
"url": "https://www.itrockstars.co.uk/",
"logo": "https://www.itrockstars.co.uk/wp-content/uploads/2016/10/IT-Rockstars-Final-Logo.png",
"hasMap": "https://goo.gl/maps/NHpRcfUjrV62",
"address": {
"@type": "PostalAddress",
"addressLocality": "Aberdeen",
"postalCode":"AB10 1UP",
"streetAddress": "42 Carden Place"
},
"description": "IT Rockstars provide IT support and technology solutions for Aberdeen and the North East of Scotland",
"name": "IT Rockstars",
"telephone": "01224 516055",
"geo": {
"@type": "GeoCoordinates",
"latitude": "57.1443103",
"longitude": "-2.1266485"
},
"sameAs" : [ "https://www.facebook.com/itrockstarsuk",
"https://twitter.com/ITRockstarsUK",
"https://www.youtube.com/user/goldmercury", "https://www.linkedin.com/company/10898436",
"https://plus.google.com/+ItrockstarsUk"]
}
</script>
```

IT Rockstars homepage including JSON local schema markup

I believe this is one of the elements to having a top ranking website in the map pack.

There are not many that know about this method and sites I've tested with always rank in the top three positions within the map pack.

Another markup we can include is the review rich snippet.

```
Results for: Review schema generator
<!-- Add this code to Review page: -->
    <div itemscope itemtype="http://schema.org/Review">
        <meta itemprop="description" content="Over the New Year, our system was down and our usual IT support was unavailable so we called IT Rockstars.
Although it was a New Year public holiday, Scott Millar from IT Rockstars was at our office within an hour, and quickly diagnosed and fixed several problems
which had caused the system failure.   He then came back the following day to assist with another IT issue.   Nothing was any bother to him and he just worked
to solve the problems calmly & efficiently.    I cannot recommend IT Rockstars highly enough - we depend on our IT systems  and IT Rockstars proved
themselves to be professional, expert and very dependable!">
        <meta itemprop="datePublished" content="now">
        <link itemprop="url" href="https://www.itrockstars.co.uk/reviews" rel="author"/>
        <a itemprop="url" href="https://www.itrockstars.co.uk/reviews"><span itemprop="name" style="display:block;"><strong>Review</strong></span></a>
        <span itemprop="reviewBody" style="display:block;">Awesome service</span>
            <span itemprop="author" itemscope itemtype="http://schema.org/Person" style="display:block;"><span itemprop="name">Zenith Resources</span></span>
    </span>
```

The review rich snippet can help drive the click-through ratio of your website in the search as a user will gravitate to the stars within the search.

Using it wisely.   It's worth noting at this stage that Google's guidelines state that the code you inject onto a page should also include the information visible on the page for the user.

This means that if you're using the review rich snippet, you must have the actual review visible to the user.   A dedicated page to customer testimonials on your site would form the basis of generating review rich snippets.

Final thoughts on the map pack.

Similar to searches with local intent "IT support near me" the map pack is going to become even more critical over time.   This is due to devices like Amazon Alexa, Google Home and other "smart" enabled devices.

When searches with local intent are used, the map pack listings is one of the top data sources a relevant answer is going to be structured on.

With the introduction of Google My Business posts, ability to reply to customer reviews it's important that you keep on top of your business listing.

If you want to take things to the next level, consider hiring an accredited Google Street View photographer. They will come to your business location and create a virtual tour of your offices/facilities. This can help users get a feel for your business and can also be fun including Easter eggs in the tour. You can find your nearest Google accredited street view photographer on this page:
https://www.google.com/streetview/hire/
https://www.google.co.uk/streetview/hire/

Chapter checklist:

- Optimize your Google business listing
- Preform a citation audit - clear up incorrect listing
- Research and add to new citation sources
- Include JSON injection in your website

Chapter 9: Backlinks

Referring backlinks (links to your website from other websites) has always been an important ranking factor. It used to be the more referring links you had, the higher your website ranked for a given term in the search.

This is still true for large popular websites. However, down at the local business level the quality of your links is far more critical than the number of links. In fact, having too many links can lead to your ranking factor reducing if the quality is not up to scratch.

What makes a quality link?

Many factors make a quality link back to your website. As a general rule of thumb, Google is looking at trusted websites. What's the overall authority of that site? Is it a reputable source? Unfortunately, we have no way of knowing how Google makes these assumptions, but it comes down to common sense.

A website that's a week old with thin content and minimal pages is more than likely not going to be trusted.

However, a local government, school or public organization that has a website for 10+ years would be classed at the top end of an authority website.

Authority

Here's a list of what I'd class as authority websites that should be targeted by IT companies looking to gain a backlink:
- University/College
- Non-profit/Charity
- Public/Governmental
- Business Network/Chamber
- Local Newspaper/Radio/TV

Once you've got some target websites, how do you go about getting a link from these sites? It's not easy, and there's a whole process call <u>backlink outreach</u>.

This is the act of gaining a link from another website site. There are various ways of doing this, but it all comes down to the creativity of how you go about it. Sponsor a local charity? Ask for a link from their website.

Support a local event or activity? Make sure the organizer includes a backlink to your website on their site.

Does your local council run a what's on page on their site? Host an event that will get listed in this and get a backlink.

Run a small radio or newspaper ad, ask for a link on the site as part of the deal.

Of course, the best type of link is from a local college/university or government website. These are highly authoritative websites.

It can be a real challenge to get a link from one of these types of institutions, but it can be done. If you can obtain a link for one of these sources, then your website will be ready to rock the search, and you will notice a jump in traffic to your site. Your website will look more reputable to Google, and it will then start to appear for more search terms.

Outreach does take time. My advice is to do a little often. Over time this activity will pay off.

Local

The other type of links that you should be targeted as an MSP/IT business is local links. These are links from local online sources relevant to your area. This helps keep your backlink profile as natural as possible. Having the local element will make sure your website appears in the search for keywords being search with local/location-based intent behind them.

Search: "Who recovers data near me."

This search has local intent but does not specify the location. With devices like Amazon Alexia and Google Home, these types of searches are becoming ever more popular.

Google's smart enough to know what the intent is and will pull up locally relevant sites. If you build locally relevant backlinks, then you've solved a big piece of the challenge with your website's appearance in local based searches.

Businesses in your local area can help with achieving this task. If you've done work for another local business and have a good relationship, ask them for mention and backlink on their website. You don't get what you don't ask for.

Similarly, you'll find other local websites that may have no relation to you but might be a good source or referring traffic. Where I'm based here in Aberdeen, Scotland we've got a ferry service that goes out to the Shetland Isles. For example, the ferry service has a local Aberdeen business directory on their website. This has been built for people visiting the local area, - the perfect place to list your business and website address.

You'll also find other business directories, try and find out who owns and runs these. If the owner is local try and strike up a relationship to obtain a free link or a more prominent link on their website.

Competitor

It can be tough to figure where to go for these authority links and locally relevant links. What makes it even harder is that when you have figured this first bit out, you then have to try to obtain the link. This is where your competitors can help.

SEO tools like Ahrefs, Majestic Backlinks, and Moz File explorer are backlink tools that will allow you to look at where your competitor, (or anyone else for that matter), is getting their backlinks from. My preference of the three tools is Ahrefs as it seems to give the most data behind a website.

Simply take the top 10 list of competitors that appear high in the search results for your most significant/competitive keyword terms (IT Support etc.). Load them into Ahrefs, and you'll have a complete list of where your competitors are getting their referring links from.

I always make this the first task in link building. Your challenge here is to match the link profile of the entire competition and exceed it with the backlink outreach process we're discussing here. These steps combined with killer content will give you an unbeatable advantage.

You can take this a step even further and load up similar local businesses' websites into Ahrefs and look at their backlink profile. From here you'll find some hidden gems of referring sites you'd never thought of when trying to obtain a backlink.

Social Fortress, Parasites, Industry Associations

The final backlink source is known in the SEO industry as a social fortress.

Social media websites like Facebook, Twitter, LinkedIn all have excellent authority in Googles eyes. The search giant knows these websites well and trusts them. They have a very high domain authority (DA). You can leverage this domain authority for your website by building your social fortress.

If you've got a Linkedin company page, twitter page, and Facebook page already make sure you have the backlink to your website listed in the profile. This is the basis of a social fortress.

The social fortress task has been made easy for us with an excellent tool called Knowem (knowem.com). Simply put your company name into Knowem's search on the front page, and the tool will go off and check the most popular authoritative social media websites across the entire internet. It will list all the social websites with high domain authority where your company name is available to register as an account.

The next step is securing your company account name on each of these sites. It takes some time to work through this step because it includes creating an account, entering company details including name, address and website URL. Where there's the option to include descriptive text on the account that will be publically viewable, it's worth using alternative text for each site. Don't just copy and paste the same description over and over to each website. This will give each account more opportunity to make it to the search results when someone enters your company name as a search term.

Increasing your brand visibility online. It will also minimize any duplicate content penalty that Google does employ (Panda Algorithm).

Part of the social fortress also include high domain authority websites that don't come under the list of "social web2.0 sites". These are sites that rank highly in the search for terms closely related to your business.

There's a great tool called SERPwoo (covered extensively in the measuring results chapter) which can help you find ideal parasite web properties.

Working in the search if you enter your competitor's company name into Google and scan the first 3-5 pages of results you'll find a treasure trove of high authority websites where you can set up your page and enter company info.

When it comes to parasite SEO, it's not all about having a link to your website. You'll find a lot of these high--ranking parasite properties won't allow you to include your URL when creating a listing/page. In which case this is your opportunity to use some of your most choice keywords that will increase the relevancy of your brand name. These parasite websites can rank on their own quite easily for longer tail searches where there's little competition.

When I first started repairing ipads in my brake fix days, there was no local web presence from my competitors for "iPad repair" and similar. I filled the search with high ranking authority sites and used the web juice from their sites to take advantage of the low competition.

Anchor text

Anchor text is the actual text that is used in the URL link to your website. There are five categories:
- **Branded: your company name**
- **Naked: the bare URL of your site/page**
- **Generic: Words like: visit website, click here, etc**
- **Keyword: A targeted keyword associated with your product/services**
- **Images/Media: Image on another website with a link to your site.**

You could quite easily beat everyone in the search results with your keyword term as your anchor text before 2012. Then came along Google's Penguin algorithm which is still in operation to this day. It effectively monitors the ratio of the five different types of anchor text. If the ratio looks unnatural (you've tried to game it with a target keyword), Penguin will kick in, and your site will lose rank for the associated keyword.

Due to this algorithm, it's just not worth gaming the system. The anchor text ratio is something that no one can gets right as it's different for every search and industry. There are just too many factors at play. So, don't try and game your SEO backlinks using anchors. Keep user interaction in mind with the page. What makes sense to include as your anchor text from the users' perspective. What's most helpful for them.

Link building, in general, does still work but there's less time associated with it due to just how smart Google has become. My last piece of advice on the topic is building links naturally. Create great content and people will want to link to you.

If you are finding that no matter what you do you can't seem to come up on the first page for a given search topic. First have a look at the search, who is your competition. Be realistic here. If it's a high domain authority website, for example, you are trying to rank for "Office 365 support" then there's just no chance you'll ever rank for a term like that when competing against Microsoft.

Realistically, it can be anywhere from 4-6 month before you'll make it to a semi-permanent position in the search results for a given keyword or topic. Of course, Google is always testing pages to see which ones perform better for its users so over time your position will change. I've had some sites enter the top 3 positions for highly competitive terms and stay there for years with no update on the content or freshness. Other times I've gained the top position too quickly, lose the rank and get kicked off to the 2nd page.

What I've learned from this experience is that a lot has to do with the competition you are up against when it comes to a particular search term. The best way to win is by implementing the tactics outlined here, and when you've tried but still can't succeed, outsmart the competition by going after other keywords they've not even thought about.

Chapter Checklist:
- Research authority link opportunities
- Run a competitor analysis for ideas on link opportunities
- Build a social fortress
- Keep your anchor text profile natural

Chapter 10: Website Layout

When I was thinking of writing a book about SEO for IT businesses, I realized that website layout and the flow of your website are just as essential elements when it comes to converting website visitors to qualified leads.

You might have the best SEO and be able to pull in thousands of visitors with your social media activities, but if the layout of your website sucks, then it's a bit like pouring water into a bucket with holes. That water leaking out of the bottom is the website traffic that could potentially be converted into phone calls and emails, but due to the poor design, it's just not happening.

The following are excerpts of an interview I recorded with Mathew Rodela of Techsite Builder for the IT Rockstars podcast. Note: Techsite builder is a bespoke WordPress based system which is offered exclusively to IT businesses as a go to turnkey website solution. I was lucky enough to spend an hour chatting with him.

Here's the interview:

Scott:

Matt, what are the primary pages I would need on my website site and why?

Matt:

Many people try to overcomplicate their business website because your business is your baby and you want to talk about all the different services you provide and be excited. This includes talking about your team and your location and your history and all that stuff. So really you want to put yourself in your client's shoes. Also, what is important to them and what are they going to want to know.

The basics:
    Homepage
    Services page
    Contact page
    Page with social proof
    Blog/Company news

My number one piece of advice is don't try to be smart or different just for the sake of being different.

I know some people try to get creative with their design a trend nowadays is to have a hamburger 3 line menu that you see on a mobile phone have that as part of your main website too, so you're not cluttered with the navigation menu you have to click that button first to see it.

I'm a big proponent of the fewer clicks your customers have to make to get to the information they need the better.

I would have the traditional horizontal navigation menu at the top of your website.

You want to feed into visitors' expectations of what a website should look like. That way they're not trying to think extra hard to find what they need to see.

They know that typically a website has a navigation menu at the top.

It's just a matter of keeping it simple.

Those four or five pages that I mentioned were the main pages you want would probably be what you'd put up in the navigation menu.

I'm not a big fan of drop-down menus.

People get confused if they hover over a menu item should they click on the main menu item? Alternatively, should they try to find what they're looking for in the dropdown and then that can lead to confusion.

Scott:

Is there anything that you'd maybe implement or suggest on how the menu should look on a mobile device?

Matt:

That hamburger menu does work well on a mobile device, and that's where it would work. You're right on mobile phones real estate is premium. So to truncate the menu down to you know a button or something is perfectly fine.

Scott:

Is there anything that you would do with the "about us" page any suggestions or advice there and how that how that should look?

Matt:

I would encourage you to be friendly and personal on the about page put a picture of yourself and your team.

Pictures of faces are always the best type of image to have on your website especially if it's actually you and not just some generic stock photo of a tech in a server room.

The best place to have it is on the About page because people are going there specifically to learn more about the business you want to connect with a person and not a company.

Tell the story of the company as if you're having a conversation with a buddy over a beer.

Scott:

The image of yourself on the homepage page. What type of image should we use? A professional looking image or is it something more casual?

Matt:

I would encourage you to put a picture on there as close as possible to what your client would see if they were to meet you in some business environment. If you wear a suit and a tie when you visit your clients if that's the kind of business you have then be formal in a suit and tie on the picture.

You set the expectation of who you are and what your company is.

That way when the client does see you they're not like you know that you're entirely different from the picture that they see you.

Like in the dating online dating profile of the person and then you meet him, and they're like 20 years older.

Scott:

That makes sense! It is common sense, but that's the type of thing I would get wrong and need to be pointed out to me.

Matt:

As you mentioned it's common sense, but it's the stuff that people don't this think about.
I see that time, and again people just aren't doing these things because.

Scott:

What should you have on the contact us page?

Matt:

I would make sure that you have multiple ways for people to make contact.
Have a contact form.
I think it's a key to having a form there and not just an email address because people want to contact you right then and again you want to reduce the number of clicks.
I would again make it very simple ask for as little information as you need to be able to reach back out to them. Name, email and description is the very minimum you might want to throw in a phone number.
Also, of course, your address and your phone number and social media links are a good thing to put on this page as well.

Scott:

Do you condone the use of a pop-up or chat box on your website?

Matt:

I do like the chat boxes I think chat boxes are great. I have had much success putting a chat box on the Techsite Builder website because many people have questions when they visit your site and you can't ever anticipate every question and answer it on the site itself.
Having that box pop up they can immediately ask you a question and then you can answer it.

Scott:

I find it interesting that you're saying that there are many questions that come through from having a chat box. I guess that can give you an idea of the type of website visitors and the type of questions that they've got in their head.
Could the answers to those questions be the basis of website content?

Matt:

Exactly and some people are in just such a hurry that they don't even want to bother looking for an answer to the question they want to talk to somebody.

Scott:

How should you guide a visitor through your website? I know this is sometimes called user flow?

Matt:

You want to think about how people will land on your website on different pages. They won't necessarily land on the home page. It could be a blog post could be or about page or some other page.

The first thing is you want to make sure that every page on your website has a way for people to contact you.

Have your phone number and maybe even a list of services on the site in the sidebar or something. Display those critical pieces of information on every page of your website.

That way it's there, and people can see it.

Whatever key piece of information do you think is required that you want new people to know about you.

Scott:

You mentioned there your telephone number on every page. Would you have that at the top of the site or the bottom or both?

Matt:

I like to have it at the top just because that way it's always visible. I know when I visit service companies' websites, and I'm doing some research, and then I'm like okay this looks like a place I'd like to do business with. Sometimes I have to go hunting for the phone number.

I might have to click through to the contact page before I find the phone number.

Whereas if it's in the header and put it in the footer you know put it both places that way if someone's first using a page they see it if they scroll down to the bottom of the page they'll see it as well.

Another thing about user flow is I like to provide a call to action. At the end of every single page of the website.

Scott:

What would that call to action be?

Matt:

I like buttons. So I want to have a button at the bottom of every page and have it be tailored to that page.

Every page should have a call to action at the bottom because you don't know when someone is going to be ready to take action. Regularly going to be after they've consumed the content on a specific page. So when they get to the bottom of the page having a button right there prompting them to take action.

Will be more likely for them to take that action to get at conversion as opposed to just relying on them to take the action.

Scott:

What questions have I not asked yet that may be important?

Matt:

Sometimes I see on other websites people have like their Facebook feed all the stuff they post on Facebook in a little box.

Alternatively, they'll have badges of all the different certifications they have shown up on every page on the sidebar or something.

You can show off your certifications on one or two pages maybe the "about page" is an excellent place to put that.

Also, if there is a relevant certification for a particular service then like if you have a Cisco certification you could put that on your networking services page.

However, you don't need to put that on every page. It just clutters things up.

Also, those Facebook feeds. Number one they can slow the site down because it's got to go to Facebook to pull that in. Number two it's taking people away from your page. If they see one of those posts in a feed then they'll go off to Facebook and then, of course, they'll get distracted.

You want to keep people on your website until they're ready to hire you or contact you or sign up for your email.

I think this is important for people because you could say you could be paying for Facebook ads or you could invest much time in search engine optimization, and you can have quite good traffic your website, but you might be losing customers phone calls just because of those holes in your site.

Scott:

I think we may be covered quite a few of them here today. I appreciate your time.

How can people get in contact with you?

Matt:

You can head over to techsitebuilder.com that has you know a contact form you can reach out, and you can learn more about tech site builder.

Scott:

Okay well, thanks for being on the show today. Appreciate it. I'm sure we'll catch up soon.

Matt

Yeah, much fun. Thanks for having me.

Chapter Checklist:
- Common sense applies
- Don't try and be clever on your website
- Keep the user experience at top of mind for site layout.

Chapter 11: Adwords

Paid advertising in the search can be a great way of increasing traffic to your website. However, there can be some nasty surprises, and it's very easy to get it completely wrong as an IT provider.

The first time I attempted to get into Google AdWords I failed. Blowing through a substantial amount of cash with nothing to show.

In this chapter, I'll be laying out how not to make the same mistakes I made and how you can use AdWords to be one of your competitive advantages.

Professional Adwords agencies will charge an arm and a leg and tell you that to have a successful AdWords campaign that has measurable results you'll need to spend anywhere from $3,000-$5,000. This is true.

Now I know many MSP's where this figure seems ???. However, I am also aware of a large number of IT who feel this amount is just a laughable. What's the solution?

Start small and refine your AdWords campaigns over time.

<u>Funnel position</u>

First, let's talk about the type of lead you're going to attract if paying for ads in the search. Ask yourself this question, what ultimately would someone be searching for that requires them to take immediate action when they arrive on your website? For an IT provider this could be many things, here are 3 examples:

1) Systems failure, a complete outage of services, P1!
2) Virus/ Ransomware outbreak.

3) Switching IT provider due to lackluster service.

These three items are what I've experienced in sales as the top three reasons why a local business is going to need immediate service and is willing to take some form of action when they land on your website.

You're going to choose only one of these scenarios for your first campaign and over the course of six months you will refine it in the Adwords system. Once you've improved it, you can move onto the other scenarios. Remember: Start small and you won't have to blow through $5000 a month before seeing results.

Brand

The other paid search terms to be targeted are your brand terms. This is covered extensively in the **Brandjacking** chapter, but you should be bidding on your brand terms. Why?

1) It helps you to dominate the search for your company name.

2) You can control the messaging when someone types your company name in the description. This is not always possible on your homepage title tag.

> Desktop
>
> **This is the ad title | Your copy here**
> Ad www.example.com
> Description

3) Keeps out any competitors that might have read this book, more specifically the **Brandjacking** chapter!

4) Branded terms cost peanuts, and you'll receive a good quality score due to click through rate.

Let's get down to work on working within a budget

Match

When you are targeting keywords in Adwords there are different ways you can do it. Let's say for example the keyword you're interested in targeting is: ransomware recovery in London.

There are three ways you can tell Adwords to display your ad. They are: Exact Match; Phrase Match; and, Broad Match.

Exact match is when someone types exactly the words. For example: "Ransomware recovery in London".

Phrase Match is when the words are part of the search. For example: "who does ransomware recovery in London".

Broad match is when someone types into the search something that is similar to your keyword. For example: "virus removal somewhere in London".

Out of the three different modifiers you only want to be working with exact match and phrase match. You'll lose too much money on board match due to your ad appearing many times on loosely related searches which are not your target audience.

Geolocation (radius)

If you're an IT business, more than likely your clients are local. Yes, there's remote support, but when working with companies, this step can quite easily be overlooked.

This, of course, will mean if there's a new business expanding into your local catchment then they'll never see your advertising. That's when your SEO has to be on point.

Schedule

Scheduling your ads to appear at the right time of the day is also something else that can keep your AdWords budget manageable. I see so many local IT firms that skip this step.

Simply put, you should have your ads displaying when your office is open. So, if a visitor to your website does take an action, (i.e., telephoning you), then it's far more likely that you'll have an opportunity to speak with them.

The other benefit of scheduling your ads to specific times of the day is that your advert will appear higher in the search. Any competitors that may also be running ads will be running 24 hours - 7 days a week. When your ads are triggered, you'll have gone through less budget which makes it more likely Google give you the higher position.

Split Test

Split testing your ads is a MUST. It is running one ad up against another and then researching which one performed better in the search. People are more likely to click one ad which will lead to more conversions on your site.

Here's an example of a split test:

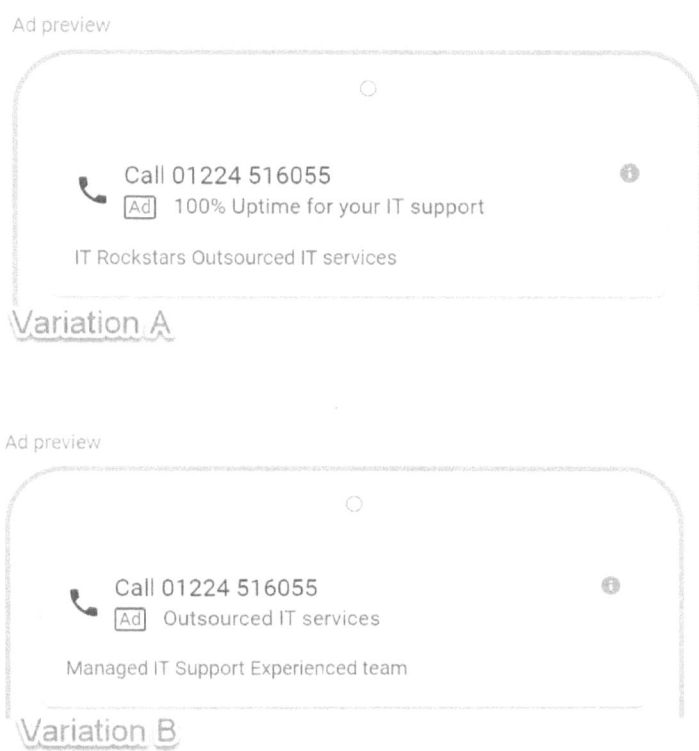

Over the course of a week run these ads in tandem. At the end of the week look up the stats and see which advert got more clicks. Also, keep in mind to take the impressions into account when deciding on this. Once you have your winner, it's time to start the process again.

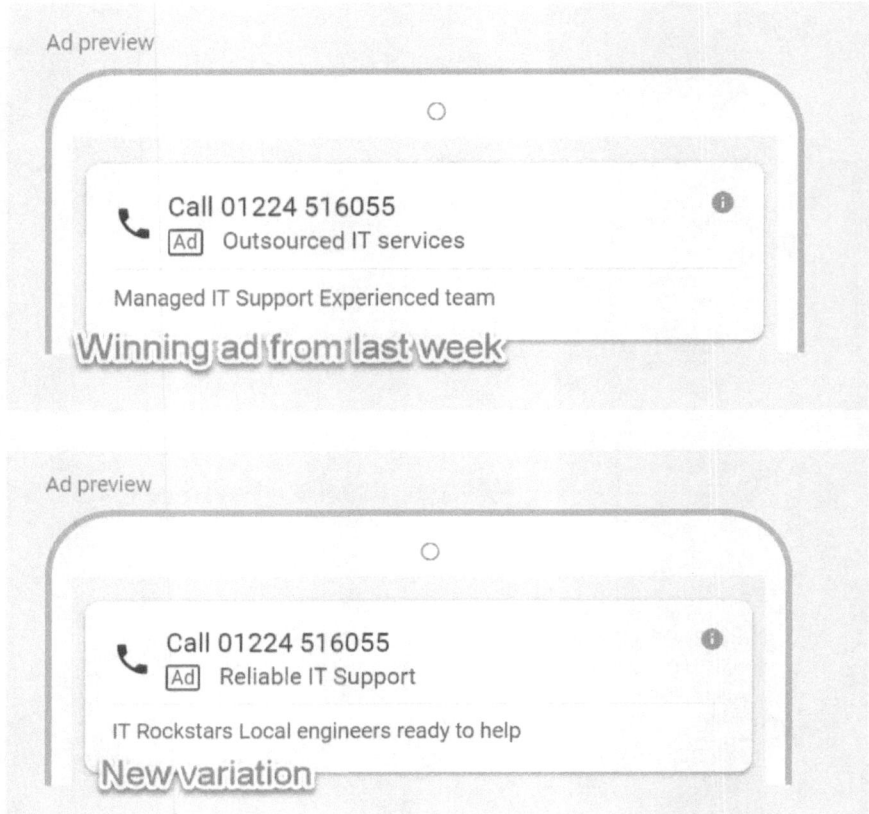

Can you outperform last week's winning ad?

The whole point of this is to make your ads optimized in the AdWords system. If people are more likely to click your ads, then Google is more likely to display your ads. Thus, giving you a higher ranking.

Quality Score

There are two different camps on quality score. Best practices state that having a good quality score matters a lot. Over time if your advert has a good quality score, you pay less for your ads to be shown. This makes perfect sense as your ad is more relevant in the search. That's the whole point of quality score.

However, the second camp believes that you should take quality score with a pinch of salt. Mainly this is down to the fact that you can have an advert with a low-quality score that will appear in the search.

You might pay more for the advert to be shown but it leads to more conversions on your website due to the way the wording is crafted within the ad.

Personally, I'm in the first camp here - follow best practices that Google outlines. You're working with a limited budget, so if you can achieve a high-quality score, then you're going to pay less for the ad.

Relevance and Landing Page

This is another biggie at which most amateurs fail. How relevant is the page that someone lands on after clicking your advert to the search they performed?

If you had an advert running for "Ransomware removal London" and linked the advert to your homepage (while this makes sense) you can be much more intelligent on where you send the visitor. You should have a page on your website for the specific purpose of someone that comes to your website after entering that term onto Google The page can talk about what ransomware does to a system and how it works. Then describe some of the processes your MSP uses to remove/protect.

Finally, the call to action with a prominent telephone number and submission form. Make it clear on the page and tell the user to call or submit the form for a quick professional response within 15 minutes.

The beauty of setting up a call to action like this using AdWords is, that if you do take the advice in regards to scheduling the ad to only appear in office hours you really can make that call back to them within 15 minutes.

They'll be impressed by this fact alone, and you'll start off a new business relationship on the right foot.

Negative Words

A daily task that you'll have to do when running AdWords is to build your list of negative keywords.

These are words people are typing in that you want to exclude your ad popping up for in the search.

For instance, you may be running an ad for "ransomware removal in London". Your ad may appear in the search for "removers in London" and that would be someone typing a search looking for a removal company. The negative word in this term is "removers".

You'll find these negative searches constantly appear when you first start running with AdWords. The only way to stop them is by building list of negative keywords over time, so that your advert is not triggered. You'll have to go into the search term report on a daily basis to weed out the negative searches. At first, it's quite a fun task as you'll see some of the searches people are performing to come to your website. And, over time you'll realize just how crucial it is to keep a negative keyword list maintained as the savings can make or break a successful Adwords campaign.

Daily Prospecting

Depending on the services you're attempting to appear for in the search you might still get stuck with limited traffic, even if you have an AdWords campaign setup. This is usually due to a poor choice of keywords.

Daily prospecting involves spending money to buy data. That data is keywords you should be targeting.

The only time you want to use broad match terms is when you are daily prospecting for new keywords.

Assign a small budget and set the ads to appear for broad match. Check the search term report daily, and you'll find some interesting keywords that you'll never have thought about.

These keywords are prospects. Plug them into the Keyword Planner tool to find out an approximate volume. If it's above 0, then it's worth creating an ad group that targets the phrase and exact match of these terms.

Other locations and competitors

If you are struggling to come up with ideas for your ad text, this is where your competitors can come in handy.

Perform a search to see what their text is in the ad copy. Make this ad copy exactly the same and put it in a split test against your creative ad copy, see which ad wins and repeat the process.

Bigger and better

Another handy research tip when planning your ad copy is to look at more sizeable geographical areas (New York, LA, London).

For example, here in the UK, I might search "IT Support London". London is a big area (8.5 million people), and the competition is fierce for a spot in the paid search. I would imagine companies are paying anywhere between $30-$80 a click for this term. They'll be working with much bigger advertising budgets. More than likely they'll be spending a dedicated AdWords agency to have these ads optimized.

Repeat the same searches on a daily basis over the course of 3 months.

Take note of the same ads that keep appearing. These are the ads that have been tested to death and optimized.

Use these ads as a source of inspiration for your own ad copy and landing pages.

Some tools will automate this process to an extent, so you do not have to check over the course of a month. One, in particular, is called SEMRush which I've used in the past to find keywords to use.

Included in the resources page is a SEMRush search box where you can get some ideas for free: https://www.itrockstars.co.uk/resources

B.I.N.G.

-- Because it's not Google, yeah I never knew that either!
-- IE and Edge users, you gotta love them.

Bing Ads has a great import tool available so once you've refined your Google Adwords campaign you can copy it across to Bing and run exactly the same setup on Bing. The beauty of this, (apart from interacting with Edge and IE users), is that the cost of running ads on Bing is significantly less as there's just not as much competition.

Chapter checklist:
- Bid on your brand terms
- Keep your ad targeting local and scheduled for office hours
- Maintain a negative keyword list
- Run a constant A/B split test
- Refine phrase match keywords to exact match campaigns where possible
- Maintain a focused landing page that relate to your ad.

Chapter 12: Brand Jacking

What you'll learn in this chapter (TDLR)

How to enter the mind of your competitor's potential clients.

When was the last time you purchased an electronic device or booked your next vacation without first researching the reviews and feedback online?

Almost everyone does research online before making any significant purchase online. The same is true when switching to a new IT supplier. If you've got a potential opportunity in your sales pipeline, then it's more than likely that opportunity has searched for your company or you.

The Switcheroo

Let's imagine for a minute one of your competitors is close to winning over a new customer. That customer will be doing research online about them. You can take advantage of this research by appearing in the search results for your competitor's brand terms, names, and services.

This takes only 10 minutes

In this chapter, I'm going to show you exactly how to appear for your competitor's search terms easily with around 10 minutes of work.

How much traffic will I get?

Before we get stuck into the detail on how to do this let's take a few minutes and break down the figures on how this works.

You're never going to appear in the number one result for your competitor's brand term. Now what I mean by the brand term is their company name. However, you can appear on the first page quite easily.

There have been numerous studies on the percentage of clicks that go to the first three results in a Google search.

CTR (Click Through Ratio) of Search engine results by position:

Moz (2014) https://moz.com/blog/google-organic-click-through-rates-in-2014

Chitika (2013) https://chitika.com/2013/06/07/the-value-of-google-result-positioning-2/

Catalyst (2011) https://moz.com/blog/mission-imposserpble-2-user-intent-click-through-rates

There have been quite a few studies on the topic and there are many factors that have to be taken into account.

The most crucial number in all of these studies is by Moz who have concluded that 24.8% of clicks go to the first position in Google.

This leaves over 75% of the clicks going elsewhere on the search results. Be it in the paid ads, further down the page, or 2nd or 3rd pages.

Here's a graph of one of the most recent studies:

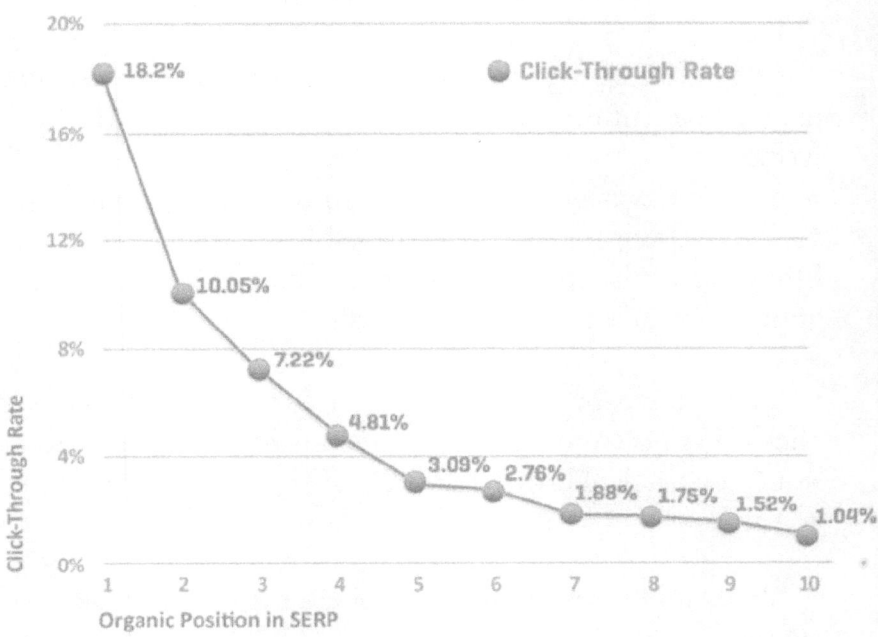

Based on this graph, let's assume we rank our website for 10% of the clicks (that's anywhere from position 5 or lower).

Let's also assume we have 5 competitors with each generating 10 opportunities per month.

We can target 10% of them with our brand jack technique. This equates to 60 qualified opportunities annually landing on our website thanks to our competitor's sales pipeline process.

Where it works well (review/alternative/owner)

Okay, so this is the secret sauce that will get you the most effective brand jack. It's back to what keywords to target and I have to thank my foray into affiliate marketing for this knowledge.

The keywords you want to go after are combination words and not just the pure brand term.

For these examples, the competitor is Scott Millar of IT Rockstars based in Aberdeen, Scotland.

Company name + location = search term would be:

"IT Rockstars Aberdeen"

Company name + review(s) = search term would be:

"IT Rockstars review"

Company name + alternative = search term would be:

"IT Rockstars alternative"

Business owner name + location = search term would be:

"Scott Millar Aberdeen"

Business owner name + company name = search term would be:

"Scott Millar IT Rockstars"

Now that we have our list of seed keywords from the examples above, we can start the process of actually appearing in the search results for these terms.

Word of advice here is to stick to between 3-5 competitors, which are ideally larger if possible.

How it works

You want to create landing pages that are optimized for these keywords but are not part of your site structure or navigation. If someone is coming to your website and sees a link to one of these landing pages, it will make no sense to them, so they should be hidden pages.

The landing page itself has to make sense for the term you are trying to rank. You can't just have your title tag as the keyword then start talking about your services.

Let's take the example of "company name + alternative"

Our on-page content would read something like this: "IT Rockstars is based in Aberdeen Scotland if you are looking to find similar companies for comparison then you've hit upon the best place to start."

Then we can list the top five (5) competitors in the area. For this example, I've listed some of my old local competition:

"Dynamic Edge"
"Simblox"
"Clark Integrated Technologies"
"Cegal"
"IT Worx"

Not only can you list the top 5 competitors, you should use this list and link internally to the brand jack page each of the competitors. This helps optimize the pages for appearing in the search results.

Lead magnet

You can then point out some pain points when choosing a new IT supplier. These pain points and the answers to solve them will be your lead magnet.

The lead magnet is a way of getting the potential customers' details in an email capture form.

"Download our guide for the 5 crucial mistakes to avoid when switching IT supplier".

Ask for the email then send to a relevant URL.

Ideally, this would be a video where you introduce yourself and cover some of the most crucial things to get right when changing IT supplier. Ending the video with a further call to action which is to schedule a time for an appointment.

The beauty of this set up is that the video is a lot more personal than a downloaded PDF, and when it comes to chasing the lead they've already met with you on video. When you call them (you've got their name and email from the lead capture) they are more likely to be responsive.

The Barnacle aka Parasite SEO

When you are building brand jacking landing pages they will take some time to appear in the search results. There is a much easier way to rank quickly and that's the barnacle.

These are other websites that appear high in the search results for brand terms and are some of the most effective ways to get on to page one of search results very fast.

This works as the barnacles have high authority with Google and are trusted websites.

Finding barnacles

The trick to finding barnacles is to keep your search niche relevant.

For IT and MSP businesses, you want to find authority websites that allow you to create pages that you can use as a brand jack landing page.

For example, I searched IT Rockstars. Out of the first 3 pages of search results I found the following barnacles. (Remember, a barnacle must allow you to create a page on their site which we can manipulate.)

Glass Door –

https://www.glassdoor.co.uk/Overview/Working-at-IT-Rockstars-EI_IE1480449.11,23.htm

Net Mums –

https://www.netmums.com/ne-scotland/local/view/local-services/website-design-and-pc-repairs/it-support-aberdeen-it-rockstars

4 Networking Biz –

http://www.4networking.biz/Members/Details/142560

You then repeat the process for each of the 5 competitors in your area to find other barnacles. If you are having a hard time finding anything, you can expand your search to more prominent brands in the IT industry that provide services to your channel.

Niche relevant examples:

> SolarWinds MSP
> IT Glue
> VM Ware

These types of searches will give you some great barnacles. As mentioned previously, it should be kept niche relevant to the IT industry. If you start looking for barnacles outside industry search terms, there is less chance these barnacles will be as effective.

Once you have a list it's just a matter of signing up for an account on each website and then creating a profile and building out the landing page.

The process itself is laborious and there's some crossover here with our local citation building, but it's such a quick win it's worth including in the checklist.

How much?

Of course, there is not only the organic search. There is also the opportunity to pay for the sponsored search. Also known as Google Adwords.

I feel this tactic is worth mentioning in this book. I have two feelings about paying for your competitors brand terms. Yes, it will get your business exposure and can provide the opportunity to generate leads for your sales funnel. However, the negative is that once your competitor finds out about your tactics they may employ a similar course of action and start bidding on your brand terms.

This leads to an interesting situation, as you will have to start an Adwords campaign specifically for your brand terms. My main advice here is to bid on the combination keyword types and not the pure brand terms.

For example:

Create a Google Adwords campaign targeting the keywords:

> "IT Rockstars Aberdeen"
> "Scott Millar Aberdeen"
> "IT Rockstars reviews"
> "IT Rockstars alternatives"

I highly suggest a phrase or exact match. Do not use the broad match. Also, target only specific geolocation as part of a brandjacking campaign. More on Adwords can be found in the **Adwords** chapter.

Moral compass

Where is your moral compass? I know some of you will question this and may not even have reached the end of the chapter, but it does pose a good question. Should I be attempting to take business from my competitors? The world is big enough for everyone.

My answer to that is, of course, you should be attempting this strategy. You see it all comes down to the qualified lead. These are like gold dust for IT business owners and MSPs. This strategy allows you to grow your business. It's a business after all and no laws have been broken.

Or have they?

There's the issue of trademark. Smart companies trademark their business name. This is a good move, especially if this book is a success and lots of MSP's start employing this strategy. The main thing to avoid is purchasing a domain name with your competitor's trademark in the name.

Here's the low down. A company can legally use a competitor's trademark or brand as necessary to fairly and accurately describe its products or to fairly and accurately compare its products and services to those of the competitor.

What it cannot do is market in a way that leads to a likelihood of consumer confusion about the source or affiliation of its products or its competitor's products. See https://www.law.com/insidecounsel/2011/11/08/ip-using-a-competitors-trademark-in-marketing/?slreturn=20171119160748)

The only other place where trademarks may not work is a Google Adwords campaign.

Your competitor has rights over their brand term, and they can request to have any and/or all of your AdWords campaigns stopped if you are using their trademark in your advertising.

The first time I came across this was when I was running an iPhone repair advert. The AdWords system did not even allow me to run the ad. Apple, however, does allow it. However, you have to go through a process with them. That being said, I highly doubt your competitor will oblige the same process.

You can find out more about Google Adwords and how trademarks work using the following link: https://support.google.com/adwordspolicy/answer/2562124?hl=en-GB

Final thoughts on brandjacking

Qualified leads are like gold dust in the IT Business world. They exist and it takes a lot of work to foster them. This book is about putting in that 1% extra effort. This strategy is worth employing, but please do it classy and not tacky. Always have the user in mind when you are developing your landing pages. Assist them as much as possible and don't go bad mouthing your competitors. That's just bad business.

Chapter Checklist:
- The whole chapter is optional, not for everyone but works well when your competitor is running a radio advertisement.

Chapter 13: Press Releases

If you've been in business a while, you'll already know what benefits a press release can have for your business. If you are a new business, or just starting out as an MSP, I'm sure you'll probably have a lot of questions about press releases (PR).

We're going to be covering two separate topics here:

1) What the SEO benefits are, what to do and what to avoid.
2) Fundamental questions answered when it comes to PR in general for your MSP/IT business.

SEO PR Benefits

Back in the days of backlinking and gaming the system press releases were used extensively to rank the top spot in Google for particular keywords.

It came down to the anchor text in the press release. If your PR firm was smart, they'd use a keyword as the backlink text to your website. This worked wonders due to how press releases are syndicating to many news websites. A few hundred syndicated articles all with your keyword as the anchor text and you'd be ranking top spot for your target keyword within a few days. However, this all changed with Google's Penguin algorithm.

Google was actively looking at unnatural anchor text ratios of websites. If it saw too many unusual keyword related anchors back to your site, then you'd be demoted in the search.

This is still true today. The question is how you can use online press releases to your businesses advantage for search engine optimization?

Well, it turns out the authority of these syndicated news sites that publish press releases are usually quite high. This is a good signal when looking for a backlink. An authoritative backlink will be a definite boost to your website's authority.

Stay clear of using keywords in your anchor text. Instead, use naked and branded terms.

>Naked = your website address e.g., (www.mycompany.com)
>Branded = your company name e.g., IT Rockstars

Also, if you can get away with it, include your NAP - this is your business name, address and phone number which is consistent with your other online business citations.

This strategy of branded terms linking back to your website and mentions of your business will not only increase the awareness of your company online. Google will also semantically start relating your business name and associate it with the topics you are discussing in your press release.

The main benefit is the increased online authority and brand awareness.

Because your press release is being syndicated, you'll also receive a boost of visitors to your website.

The other benefit of online press releases is that you may have dealt with an SEO agency in the past that used too many keyworded related anchors to your website.

Having branded and naked references to your website will help dilute the anchor text. Thus, improving a bad anchor text ratio footprint.

These are the main benefits from an SEO perspective a press release will have but what about your business in general? What will a PR firm offer you?

I caught up with Graeme Forbes from Precise Communications based in Aberdeen, Scotland. Graeme has worked in PR for many years and services small to medium size businesses. I met Graeme when he did PR for the MSP I worked with and also through BNI so he was well placed to answer specific questions I think will benefit you, especially if you've never gone down the PR route in your business.

With a list of questions ready to fire at Graeme, I thought why not interview him and include his answers in this book. He agreed. The following are exerts from the interview which is published on the IT Rockstars podcast.

Scott:

Why would an IT company employ a PR firm?
Graeme:

Let us flip that question on its head. Why would a PR firm hire an IT company instead of doing it themselves.? Most likely because it's not something they're an expert in. It's not something that they have time to do themselves, or it's just something that they don't have any idea of where to start.

Press releases can help you educate new and existing customers about products and services that your business sells. It's also a very cost-effective way of promoting your company which will ultimately lead to more business.

Scott:

How do you choose a PR firm?

Graeme:

First thing is the personal relationship. Find someone that you like and trust. Secondly, you want someone that has a proven track record. Particularly if you are working in a specialist area like IT.
If you have a specific aim in mind for your press releases, then you may have to be entirely accurate on the type of PR firm you employ.

Scott:

Okay so we've chosen a PR firm, what is the process, how do we get started working with them? What should we be thinking about as an IT business as we enter in to a relationship with this PR firm, what should be top of mind?

Graeme:

An effective strategy for your press release is very much a two-way relationship. Dedicate some time to this. It can't all be down to the PR firm.
That's something as simple as a monthly meeting, regular phone calls. If you go months with no communication between the two, the process will soon grind to a halt.

Accept that there's a time commitment to provide the information to the PR firm to make the campaign a success.

You'll also need to think about your primary audience. It may be that you want to speak to industry professionals. It may be that you want to talk to people in the general business community. For example, a finance director. Based on that decision, the PR firm can then work on tailoring your messaging. This would inform the level of jargon and technical information that would be communicated.

Scott:

In the IT world, finance directors are usually held as the decision makers when it comes to technology-related suppliers in the business. How would we go about targeting these types of professionals?

Graeme:

Print media is beneficial in targeting senior decision makers and executives. This is particularly true in more corporate organizations. You may want to focus on local and regional business press.

It's also a worthwhile task to identify publications that they read in their own time as well. That might be a specific industry magazine. There's a lot of choices regarding media outlets. You need to find the ones that will give you the best return.

Scott:

How much does it cost to hire a PR firm?

Graeme:

To give you an indication. It depends on the level of output and expectations that the client has. If there's more regular content, then that is going to cost more.

The size of the company influences costs. Additionally, what's the operational level? Local, regional, national or international. That's all going to impact price.

Scott:

Can I write my own press release?

Graeme:

It's not necessarily a bad thing. The clients already went to the trouble of gathering the information. Our job would be to rewrite this and decide how best to present that information.

Many PR professionals write in a media-friendly style. If you haven't worked as a journalist, you are unlikely to know what this style is. This can be as simple as capitalizing job titles to writing shorthand for expression of phrases.

Scott:

What are the side effects of a press release?

Graeme:

The Worst thing that can happen is that you spend a lot of time editing a press release and it's never used or not of interest. This can be minimized by thinking about the audience.

Sometimes it can be outside of your control, a crisis in the news, an election, etc. This will reduce the chances of your release appearing in the media.

Scott:

What should we base a press release on if I want to scale my business and increase sales?

Graeme:

Signs of company growth, you might be moving office, employing new staff or investing in technology. If there's some news angle to it.
Secondly, you want to fit in your key messaging. What's your USP, what are your essential products and services?

You would want to weave this into your press release. It has to be subtle. The first thing you need to do is have some form of a hook. Then you can reinforce your key messaging after that.
If you don't have any news at the time, it may be that you go down the route of some expert commentary.

Scott:

What questions have I missed here, Graeme, that you think may be important to an IT business owner?

Graeme:

Let's take cybersecurity as an example. That's a topic that a lot of people are worried about. They don't need a degree in IT or any level of professional competence to be worried about it.

Usually, if you are trying to position yourself as the experts on an issue that's making headlines, it's important to strip away the technical jargon and make the article as simple as possible. For example, what steps can I take now to protect myself against these types of threats? Mentioning something as simple as changing your password makes the article as universal as possible so that you are capturing a broad audience.

You also don't want to plug your products and services too much. That would turn people off to the critical message that you are trying to get across. People are quite savvy these days, and they know a sales pitch when they see one. If you are seen to being generous with your advice can help build goodwill with the audience.

End of interview.

Chapter 14: Measuring Results and Future Proofing

When you first start your journey in optimizing your website, you'll probably want to keep track of results and visitor numbers coming to your site.

When your search optimization, content planning and creation finally pays off, you will start to see more traffic coming to your site.

There will be a period when you'll be checking stats almost twice a day with the excitement of how many people are coming to your website. But checking stats on a daily basis will drive you mad in the long term, so it's not a great habit to get into. The solution to breaking this habit is by looking at the goals you set out for your website in the first place.

From an MSP's perspective, the goal is usually to educate the local online audience about how the services and technology you provide can help their business. This will, over time, make you the go-to authority on the topic and will, in the end, generate leads which turn into sales.

Measuring this goal can be challenging, but we're going to cover what data you need to be collecting to help make informed decisions about how well the content strategy, content creation, and outreach is paying off.

Hidden in the data you'll also learn where you should be providing more focus and improvements that can be made on existing content. This will help drive the next 12 months of content creation after the first year.

Google Analytics

Google Analytics (GA) is the go-to tool for measuring how much traffic is coming to your website. It can be pretty tough to navigate due to all of the data that the service collects when someone visits your site.

If you've not already got a Google Analytics account, I'd suggest signing up to one and installing the tracking code on your site ASAP. You need to be able to measure exactly what the traffic is on any given day.

I'll admit right here that I was not a fan of Google Analytics until I did a full 1-day course on advanced analytics. What you can do with this free service blew my mind. Before using it, I loved Clicky, which is another similar reporting tool for web stats. Clicky has a great user interface and is easy to navigate. However, the feature set in Google Analytics is far more powerful, and for an established business it's worth playing with the big boys.

Sorry Clicky.

Content Drill-down

The first metric I always concentrate on when generating my monthly report is what content (pages) are popular on my website. Which of the inner pages are getting the most traffic and what's the referral source of this traffic?

To get to this metric in GA go to Behaviour > Site Content > Content Drilldown

Once I know what the most popular pages are I'll look them over to see exactly what I can improve to make them even better. The next task is making sure those pages have some form of a lead magnet or call to action on those popular pages.

It makes a lot of sense that the most popular pages on your website (apart from your homepage) should have some way of capturing the visitor's details.

There's a lot of options on how you can do this, but the number one thing you should be trying to achieve here is capturing the details. What method is most likely for someone to take the required action of entering a form, entering an email or picking up the phone. Figure that one out. It may require testing over a few months to see what works. Pay close attention to how the user got to the page and what the page is about. This will help you determine what the call to action should be that converts.

What's the worst page(s) on your site and why?

Not only will the content drill down give you the most popular pages on your website but you can also view the worst pages.

Now I should probably state that a bad page may have more traffic than a good page. What makes it worse is the bounce rate, page exit number, and conversion rate.

If I'm confusing you sorry, here's a quick detail:

> Bounce rate: Amount of users that view only one page before exiting.
>
> Page Exits: Does the page promote exits of your website compared to others?

Conversion: You might be getting good traffic but is it converting to the call to action or lead magnet? You can measure that with goals. (Covered later in this chapter)

There are also pages that don't get a lot of traffic, and you'd expect them to get more. This is when we may have to look at the content, on page technical and what the competition is in the search results.

There is also the possibility that there's just not much traffic or interest in the topic your covering.

A note about popular pages:

If you've got pages that get heavily trafficked, work out what similar topics you can discuss then plan and put into your content calendar. It makes sense to build on something that is already working. This is where GA can work well. Once you find out where there's an interest you can build upon it and operate it into future content.

Network Report

The network report can be accessed via Audience > Technology >Network Report.

I've not been a massive fan of this in the past, but it can help let you know what companies are viewing your website. From a sales perspective, this can be quite useful to look at.

Simply put if you see local companies within the network report that are not already on your books then these may be prime targets for your sales team to get into contact with.

Goals

Accessed via Conversion > Goals

Having a lead magnet, call to action or form on your website where you can capture user info is a top priority. Especially once you start running PPC campaigns. You need every click to your site to be an opportunity of getting hold of lead information.

Setting up goals within GA allows you to easily see how well your pages are converting. Someone lands on your page then completes a form. If you track these steps via a goal, you can then segment over time what type of website visitor leads to a conversion.

When I first heard about goals, I thought it was a useful feature to implement to measure conversion rates, and when I realized you could segment, overtime, the path most popular that led to a conversion, it changed the way I planned out future content. It's a powerful metric and one that will get better with time if you set it up from day one.

UTM Code

The UTM (Urchin Tracking Module) code is a handy feature Google created that allows you to append URLs so that you can track the source, medium, and campaign.

This allows you to easily tell where users came from when visiting your website. Especially useful if you're dropping your links in email newsletters, social platforms, and other websites. Again, start using this from on day one, and your data reports will be spot on.

Google Webmaster tools

This is probably more important than Google Analytics from an SEO perspective. Google Webmaster tools is another must service (free) which you should have running on your website. It allows you to see where there might be problems with your website like areas that are not indexed, pages that can't be crawled by Google and if there's server hosting errors and the like.

The best bit about the whole tool is the search analytics feature. You would have guessed with a name like that it would be included in GA!

Anyway, the search analytics feature allows you to see exactly what keywords your website is appearing for. It will also tell you how many clicks you are getting and impressions in the search.

This is a handy tool to figure out what keywords you might be ranking for but just not up near the top spot. I've used the search analytics tool countless times to figure out what content could rank higher with just a quick change of the title tag on the page.

SERPwoo

I've followed a couple of the developers of this product for many years on various online forums. Some of their posts are epic insights to digital marketing in general and are worthy of mention here.

Similar to search analytics Serpwoo will tell you where your website is ranking in the search for a given keyword.

What's awesome about this tool is that it will track your rank and your competitor's rank over time, giving you a much more detailed insight to the competition you are up against in the search and what exactly is ranking and when.

This is especially useful for tracking results when starting out. You may not be appearing anywhere in the search for your target topics, but over time you'll be able to see exactly what improvements your site is making. Give it 4-6 months and Serpwoo will show just how all your effort has paid off in the great interactive dashboard that it's famous for in the SEO community.

Call tracking

Call tracking was one of my all time favorites back in the break-fix days. I used a service here in the UK called TTNC, but there are many call tracking services available both in the U.S. and everywhere else.

The way I had it set up was with a call whisper service. Every time a customer called me that had been on my website I'd get a short message before the customer would connect on the phone. The service allowed me to upload any wav file as the short message so in my wisdom I choose the Windows 3.1 startup sound.

The service gives you call tracking number that you place all over your website instead of your real number. I had the "tada" sound being played to me 20 times a day. Epic.

The call tracking feature works best when combined with GA goals. Google does offer its version of call tracking using Google Adwords. Over time you'll be able to analyze exactly what website users tend to lead to a phone call which is awesome. This is another day one activity that needs to be in place.

Future Proofing and Google Trends

Remember when cloud computing was in its infancy? IT managers and business owners alike were reluctant to make the move to BPOS / Google Apps. Heck even the IT/MSP community was split about migrating email to the cloud.

For me it seemed like a no-brainer. My personal email is in the cloud, and it's worked fine since 1995. So, why does business email have to be such a hassle?

Things have moved on from that time, and now Office 356 is the defacto solution for many business email systems.

I'm kicking myself though. I was an early adopter but did not share the enthusiasm in my blog. If I had written up articles back in 2011 about how I was on the cutting edge of IT business systems, and if I had shared this knowledge and experience it would have been beneficial for everyone.

I would have been proven right, and this would have added to my authority status.

Of course, there's no point dwelling in the past. What's to stop you starting today and educating your audience on the cutting edge, where you see things moving to for IT?

Google Trends is a tool that can help with this task. It's a unique insight into how popular topics are over time.

Here's an example of Office 365 trend:

Here's another for "IT Support":

Check out the summer dips on that one!

Okay, great tool but what can I use it for?

In the lower bottom right-hand side are "related topics." This is sorted by topics that are rising in popularity.

Here are the related topics for the topic "cybersecurity."

These are the perfect insights to what's hot just now and topics you should be writing about. Trending topics will help drive more traffic to your website.

The final tip on measuring results

Watch out for the personalized search feature Google serves up. This will skew your perception of where your website is appearing in the search.

What the personalized search does is serve up pages that you've already visited higher in the search results.

When you're checking on your page ranking, or a competitors,' its worth using a tool like SerpWoo or Google Adwords Ad preview tool to review the personalised search element.

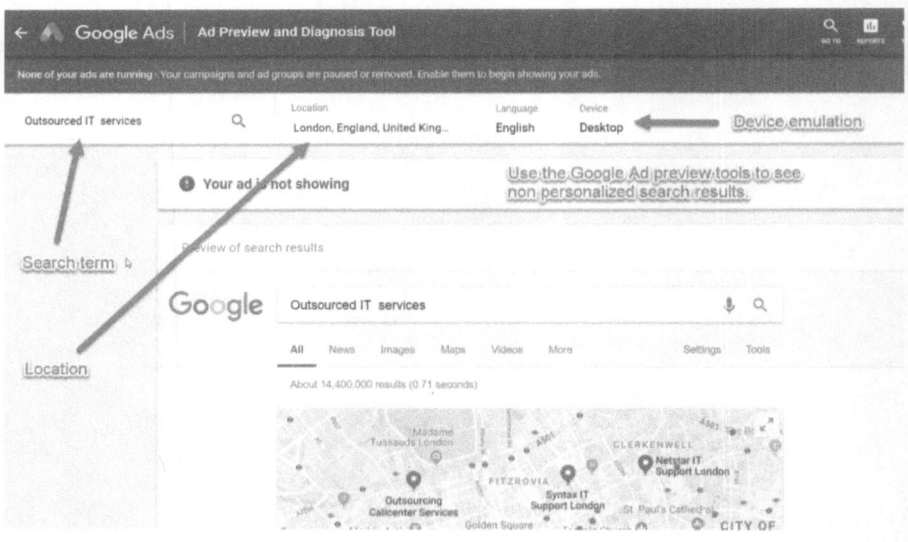

Chapter Checklist:
- Install google analytics today.
- Find the pages that are most popular, work out why and build on that with future content.
- Set up goals for your lead magnet efforts.
- Include UTM urls when promoting your content.
- Double check webmaster tools for site errors and popular keywords.

Chapter 15: Build to sell.

If you've managed to read all the way to here, you should get a medal.

There's just so much information and action points to take in.

How do you prioritize all of this book?

There are some simple steps you can do.

First get into the habit of writing content - the sooner you've knocked out ten 2000 word articles about topics your audience wants to read and engage with you'll find half the battle has been done.

The 2nd priority has to be ranking in the map pack. Mainly because it's an easy win and does not eat up too much of your valuable time.

3rd and final priority has to be your on-page SEO. Getting the technical stuff out the way fast will help with a website that you already own and have done no work on.

These three things alone will not bring SEO success but will get you started in the right direction. Remember this is very much a long-term marketing play.

Not only will the content you produce now pay divide ends off in future but when it comes time to sell your IT/MSP business you will have a highly valuable asset.

Dominating the search in 3-5 years from now is only going to become more relevant as Millenials mature into decision making positions within the local business landscape there going to come straight to Google before asking for a referral.

Like almost everything about running an IT business, the journey is tough but once you've reached a level of success the search engines will reward you.

What's still missing?

I've only scratched the surface here in regards to online marketing.

There are many powerful tools now available to a local IT business.

LinkedIn, email campaigns and even facebook re-targeting which can complement and SEO strategy for your IT Business.

If you'd like help with this whole process then my business, IT Rockstars can help you generate more qualified leads.

We've got two services available.

1) A 6-month training course that leads you through the steps outlined in this book with a monthly check in on progress.

2) Done for you content generation & promotion service. We offer white label bespoke content for your IT/MSP business website & social channels.

To discuss further contact scott@itrockstars.co.uk

Regards

-Scott Millar

www.ingramcontent.com/pod-product-compliance
Lightning Source LLC
Chambersburg PA
CBHW031417210526
45464CB00005B/1927